Praise for Breaking the Silence

Having met Shannon as she began thinking about leaving the public school system, and having worked with her closely on that plan, her exit, and the beginning of her new business and reclaimed life, I've been privileged with a front-seat for the show that never should have happened.

This book gives you a front seat, too, and shares the heartbreaks, as well as the triumphs; the unfortunate endings, as well as the inspired beginnings. It leaves you, all at once, sad and hopeful, and with a place to start a conversation, if you've a mind to, in your own community.

Shannon is a force for good in the world. It's absolutely the loss of the public education system that she's left. And it's absolutely our gain that she's shared herself so transparently and vulnerably through her beautiful memoir.

—*Anastacia Brice, Business Foundations Coach*

This is a powerhouse book filled with honest insight and courageous words which illustrate that we must stand up for what we believe in most, even when it's the difficult path. We must all become leaders in education reform. Taking the first step is the most difficult part, but without that first step, we will never see change.

—*Tim McDonald, Director of Community at The Huffington Post*

This book is a wake-up call to administrators, advocates, and parents who truly care about why we lose great teachers and how we can save good schools.

—*Tai Goodwin-Kastens, parent, author, former 5th-grade teacher*

Praise for Breaking the Silence

A must-read for anyone who is a teacher, whether you work with children or adults. Shannon doesn't sugar-coat things; she tells it like it really, truly is. An inspiring look at the impact teachers make and the reality of what goes on behind the curtain when you're making a big change in your own life.

—*Karyn Greenstreet, Small Business Coach, Mastermind Expert*

Shannon Hernandez gives a straightforward account of the problems teachers face in the American public education system today. As a European mother, whose sons attended school in the U.S., I now understand why many young, enthusiastic teachers are disillusioned and quit. With too many rigid structures in place, we forget that teaching and learning should be a joy.

—*Sonia Marsh, author of award-winning memoir,*
Freeways to Flip-Flops, *founder of the My Gutsy Story® Anthology*

Breaking the Silence will outrage and inspire anyone who cares deeply about the American educational system. It is at once a riveting tale of the heartbreaking failures of our public schools and an uplifting memoir of one woman's journey of reinvention. Read it and give it to your friends.

—*Molly Gordon, Master Certified Coach*

BREAKING THE SILENCE

My Final Forty Days
as a
Public School Teacher

BREAKING THE SILENCE

My Final Forty Days
as a
Public School Teacher

M. Shannon Hernandez

Mill City Press
Minneapolis, MN

Mill City Press, Inc.
322 First Avenue N, 5th floor
Minneapolis, MN 55401
612.455.2293
www.millcitypublishing.com

ISBN-13: 978-1-62652-962-5
LCCN: 2014911799

Editing and interior design by Bonnie McDermid
Cover photo and author photo by Carlos Detres

Ordering information
Visit my website at www.MyFinal40Days.com
www.TheWriting-Whisperer.com

Printed in the United States of America

Dedication

This book is dedicated to the superb teachers working in the trenches of public education. The daily battles you fight for our students are not fought in vain. I know the risks you take when speaking up for them and fighting for what is right in public education. I also know that many of you have been silenced with threats to your professional reputation and career advancement.

This book was written to break the silence: to invite parents, administrators, and concerned community members into our classrooms to witness the reasons why the public education system is failing our children and defeating so many good teachers. It was written to spark discussion at the local level about ways to retain good teachers—like you—who are essential to preparing our children to be thoughtful, contributing members of our society.

This book is also for those of you who are struggling in jobs or careers that are draining you mentally, physically, emotionally, and spiritually. Do not give up! You can find happiness again! I did, and believe with everything in me that you are one hundred percent deserving of living a life you truly love, each and every day.

Table of Contents

Table of Contents

Foreword

I laughed and I cried while reading M. Shannon Hernandez's memoir, *Breaking the Silence,* a chronicle of Hernandez's final forty days as a public school teacher, which eloquently shows the academic and personal successes accomplished by skilled and inspiring teachers in schools where curriculum reform has otherwise failed. Her courageous voice gives us insight into the reality and pain students and their teachers experience every day. It is a beautiful account of what public education ought to be, as well as a provocative and stirring look at why so many great teachers are leaving the field.

As a college researcher and educator of teachers, I had the privilege of working and teaching side-by-side with Shannon while she was earning her Master's in Science Education. Once I witnessed firsthand her gift for teaching language literacy, I invited her to co-teach my classes for pre-service and in-service teachers, which she continues to do today. Our college students love her passion for teaching and commitment to her students, personal attributes that are very apparent to everyone who works with her.

Yet—this dedicated and influential educator has been pushed out of public education, abandoned by a system at odds with the art and craft of teaching and permeated with callous disregard for the emotional and material needs of teachers and students.

I am all too familiar with this war on teachers. Many of the young, idealistic educators I teach enter the profession full of promise and optimism, only to be thwarted and attacked by administrators, profiteers, and politicians.

It is a great loss and a tragedy that Shannon and other quality teachers like her feel they need to leave the classroom to have a future where they are valued, appreciated, and treated like professionals. The loss of their talent affects every one of us—our children, families, communities, and our country—and denigrates our hopes for a literate and healthy citizenry.

Current discussions about education reform have notably excluded teachers from the debate. However, in *Breaking the Silence*, you will read one courageous educator speak for her students and her profession. You will become familiar with the seemingly little things in the classroom that are, in fact, critical to teaching and learning: the dichotomy between teaching children and teaching to test scores, the impact poverty and socioeconomic status have on learning, how compassion and kindness are often rejected by our current educational system in favor of undignified discipline and punishment, and why quality teachers will continue leaving education until they are accorded the respect they deserve and included as full partners in the efforts to reform public education.

Hernandez's book inspires me because it shows what is possible when students are taught by quality teachers. It also challenges me to be cognizant of the formidable hurdles our public school teachers must overcome just to do their jobs every day. And it confronts me with the need to be more active in combating current policies that hamper teachers and disenfranchise students.

This book is a call for everyone in our society to give teachers and the teaching profession the respect and honor they deserve. It is a must-read for those interested in becoming teachers and for everyone with a stake in public education—parents, educators, administrators, curriculum developers, business owners, community leaders, and politicians.

Above all, *Breaking the Silence* chronicles the reinvention of an educator's life, guided by her principles, optimism, and dreams to find personal and professional happiness once again.

Konstantinos Alexakos, Ph.D.
New York, New York
August, 2014

Preface

I have always been a big dreamer, an out-of-the-box thinker, a change agent, and an individual who refuses to be unhappy. I make decisions rooted in love, compassion, and understanding, and have never allowed myself to be a silent victim in any situation. These qualities are the foundation of who I am and what I stand for and why, after fifteen years as a public school teacher, I could no longer remain in a career that was sucking my soul dry and depriving me of personal and professional happiness.

My teaching career began at the age of twenty-one, straight out of college, in a second-grade classroom in a small town outside of Concord, North Carolina. Early in my career I thought I wanted to teach the little ones, but I learned rather quickly my personality was better suited to middle-school students. So after a few years of teaching in elementary school, I transitioned to teaching in middle school, where I remained for the next twelve years.

Throughout my middle-school years, I taught English Language Arts (ELA) and Social Studies. I coached sports teams and served as grade team leader, curriculum chair, and student teaching supervisor, mentored new teachers and initiated many programs and clubs in the schools I served in North Carolina and New York City.

I taught students firsthand how rewarding it is to learn while traveling. We took summer trips to the Grand Canyon, Canada, London, Paris, and Rome. I worked diligently every year to secure grant funds so I could have the most current literature in my classroom library. I also worked with local organizations to ensure my students could visit museums, attend plays, and have other cultural experiences so they could learn about the world around them.

After meeting my Brooklynite husband during the tenth year of my teaching career, I was ready for the adventure of city life. My first New York City teaching job was in Spanish Harlem. While some days I wondered if I would make it from the school to the train station alive, I fell in love with my inner-city students—their strengths, their struggles, and especially their big-city survival skills.

The last four years of my teaching career were in an excellent school in Manhattan. I had never taught with a more dedicated and unified staff. The students were also some of the most kindhearted and intelligent I had had the honor of teaching.

Upon accepting a teaching position in New York City, I was well aware I would need to return to college and earn my master's degree, as this is a certification requirement for this state. I enrolled in Brooklyn College and began working towards a degree in Biology Education. I also knew that I would be losing the tenured position I had worked so hard to earn during my first ten years of teaching in North Carolina. While I wasn't thrilled about the latter point, because it meant, once again, "proving" myself to a new school district, I accepted it. Within three years of teaching in New York City, my tenure had been granted to me once again.

It was in October of 2012, when Hurricane Sandy blew through our area, that two pivotal pieces of information were revealed to me, changing the course of my life and career. First, I had just been informed by the New York City certification department that I would lose my tenure, again, once I began teaching under my new biology certification the following fall.

I was livid. I cried. I screamed. I made phone calls. And with each person I spoke to, the news was consistent: Because I was switching from a certification in ELA to Biology, my tenure would be taken from me, and I would have to prove, once again, that I was a teacher worthy of keeping.

The second piece of information that changed the direction of my life was revealed to me in my journal during this same week. Because the public schools were being used as emergency shelters for people who had been displaced by Hurricane Sandy, the employees and students were granted a week off from our normal routine. I have always been an avid journal writer, and I was using my journal as a tool to make sense of the destruction and sadness I was witnessing in our area. Because I was still bitter and raw about the tenure situation, pieces of that were also sprinkled throughout the pages.

I woke up on the fourth day of my unexpected week off and took out my journal. I read the previous day's entry. What emerged on that page—one tiny sentence—changed my life. I had written, "I deserve to be happy again." As I read that statement, it lodged itself in my heart, and tears spilled down my cheeks. I was sitting at the kitchen table in my Brooklyn apartment, sobbing, tears streaking the ink on the pages. How had I not realized before now just how unhappy I was in my career?

My husband, who was working from home that day, watched all of this emotion unfurl. He knew that I was sick and tired of working in a system that didn't appreciate me for the teacher I was, and he knew I was struggling terribly with my personal happiness. I remember walking over to his desk, embracing him in a hug, and saying between sobs, "Babe, I have to find a way out of this career. I don't know how I'm going to do it, but I can't return to the classroom next fall." He hugged me even tighter, and said the four most powerful words that still bring tears to my eyes, "I will support you."

The next three months were a flurry of activity and a combination of deep reflection, creative thinking, and making moves to get my exit strategy together. I decided that I would open a business in the beginning of 2013, teaching business owners how to write better content for their audiences, as well as helping them tell their own personal stories through digital storytelling. I named my company The Writing Whisperer, and brought on a team of people who were successful in various parts of business, so they could help me build my new dream and prepare for my launch in February.

This may have been one of the most stressful and sleep-deprived times in my life, but I knew I was on the right track because I was happy and excited about my future again! Most days I woke up at 3:00 in the morning and worked on graduate school projects until 6:40, when I left my house and boarded the train to Manhattan. Once I arrived in my classroom, I devoted all of my heart, energy, and focus on my students. When the final bell rang at 3:20, I packed my bags, walked out of the building, got on the train, grabbed a quick forty-minute nap, and headed to my evening college classes. When I finally arrived home at 9:00 at night, exhausted by a full day of work and graduate-level study, I devoted two hours to building my business.

When February of 2013 came around, The Writing Whisperer was ready to launch. Somehow, I had also, despite my hectic, sleep-deprived schedule, graduated with a 4.0 grade point average in my master's program! Deep within my soul, even before I had my first client, I believed at my core I would be a successful business owner, which would allow me to chart my own course in life, and never have to prove to anyone else, ever again, that I was "good enough." These are the thoughts that fueled me when uncertainty and fear crept into my brain.

In March, the decision was made. I told the administration that I would not be returning the following year. I also decided to write a journal about my emotions surrounding my departure from the world of public education after so many years of teaching. Forty days out from my resignation date, I opened up my notebook and jotted down the daily stories that unfolded in Room 719.

Those notes became the book you are holding today—a true account that chronicles my final forty days as a public school teacher—the good, the bad, and the utterly inexplicable.

Acknowledgements

I am forever grateful to many people for their guidance in my life, my teaching career, my transformation from teacher to business owner, and the writing of this book…

To my husband, Michael, who has supported my journey in finding true happiness, and thus, has spent many nights alone while I have been building my business or in self-imposed seclusion so I can continue to write and inspire my readers.

To my parents, William and Linda Spray, and my sisters, Julie and Kristi, who continue to champion me in standing up for what I believe in and going after the dreams in my heart.

To my business coach, Anastacia Brice, who believed in my dream of building a business and a new life for me, even before I fully believed it could actually happen.

To my entire business support team (especially my Virtual Assistant, Sandy Wiles), who work day in and day out behind the scenes of The Writing Whisperer, ensuring that my company continues to reach new heights, so that I have the freedom and space I need to live a life I love.

To Konstantinos Alexakos, my colleague at Brooklyn College, who has given me countless words of encouragement since the day I shared with him my decision to leave the public school system.

To Andrew Sullivan, Nancy Barkemeyer, and Chuck Borders, three of my former administrators, who continue to lead their school communities by putting love and understanding first.

To my former teaching colleagues, who feed me massive doses of courage so I can keep writing and breaking the silence, even when hints of uncertainty and fear creep in.

To Angie Buescher, my former English teacher, who provided me with constant guidance and inspiration during my high school years, and inspired me to pursue an education degree and hone my craft as a writer.

To Ann Eaves, my first mentor, who taught me the value of building a community of caring and compassionate citizens in the classroom.

To my editor and project manager, Bonnie McDermid, who is one of the most detail-oriented and pleasant people I have ever had the privilege of working with.

To my photographer, Carlos Detres, whose vision captured everything this book stands for, in one single shot, and to all the individuals at Mill City Press who brought my book to life.

To my beta readers, who volunteered to critique my manuscript (on very short notice), whose critical reading, feedback, and insight helped mold the final version.

To my current and former students, who enrich my life more than they will ever know, and who continue to inspire me each time a new message appears in my inbox.

And last, but certainly not least…

To you, my reader, who already possesses everything within you to live a life of true happiness and bliss, each and every single day.

Introduction

This memoir offers three themes that will touch different people at different times in their journeys.

First, it's a story of love. The words in this book show my passion for teaching and how much I valued the thousands of students I had the privilege to work with and learn from during my career as a public school teacher.

Second, it's a story of loss. As you read the intimate vignettes I share, it will become quite clear how horribly the public education system fails our nation. The students are losing their right to a quality, well-rounded education, and the system is losing superb teachers who refuse to stay in a broken, harsh, and uncaring environment. This story is also about the loss of a dream—the dream of teaching in a classroom—which I had had since the age of seven. This breaks my heart, and I hope it breaks yours, too.

Finally, it's a story of hope and self-empowerment. This memoir highlights what can happen when you focus on your dreams and stand in your truth. I was desperately seeking a life filled with love and compassion, meaning and purpose. The moment I decided to make bold moves and plan my exit from my job as a teacher was when I found personal and professional happiness once again.

As you read the story of my final forty days in the classroom, I encourage you to interact with the text. On the pages following my story are ideas for deeper reading and discussion. I am certain, no matter if you are reading this book because you have a stake in the future of our nation's children, or are seeking a more positive, fulfilling future for yourself, you will find much value in these suggestions.

For teachers:

- Discover the stories that resonate most with you as a classroom leader. Keep a daily journal of your own so that you, too, can reflect on the sweet interactions you have with your students. Learn from those circumstances in which you might react differently next time, allowing you to grow, personally and professionally.

- Use this book as a discussion starter. Gather together a group of teachers to explore how to infuse more compassion, understanding, and valuable life lessons into the curriculum.

- If you feel you have lost your passion for the profession, use the words in this book to help you reconnect with your "Why?" for staying in the classroom or to help you connect with your inner voice that is telling you it's time to leave.

- Use the resources at the back of this book to find an organization so you can become more involved in the education reform movement. Your voice matters!

For administrators:

- As a school leader, many responsibilities and tasks weigh on you daily. I encourage you to read this memoir through the lens of your role in shaping the overall school tone and environment. Which stories reflect the atmosphere of your school building the most? What is working well toward create a positive school tone and what needs to be refined and revamped?

- Use this book as a school-wide tool for professional development. Consider starting a book club in which you use the stories as a way to spark discussion. Poll teachers on their feelings concerning curriculum, the current practices and policies in place, school tone, and the overall value and appreciation they feel working for you as a building leader. Use the information gleaned from the discussions and work collaboratively with the staff to enhance the overall school ecosystem.

- Utilize the resources at the back of this book to discover innovative ways you can facilitate leadership through more compassion and understanding, increase the quality of dialogue among your staff, and improve the overall school culture.

For parents:

- As you are well aware, your work is far from done when your children go to school. Schools need the support of parents in more ways than you could ever imagine. Use the stories in this book to understand the many activities teachers create to enhance the everyday curriculum. Then, visit your child's school and ask how you can become more involved in the many initiatives and activities which are currently being planned.

- Mark the passages in the book that illustrate the behind-the-scenes work your child's teachers are doing, day in and day out, and are most likely going unnoticed. Write frequent, heartfelt letters of gratitude and appreciation to teachers; those letters are highly valued and mean more than you could ever imagine.

- Your voice in education reform carries much weight. Use the resources at the back of this book to locate a reform organization with which you can become more involved.

For teacher preparation programs:

- As I continue working closely with student teachers at the college level, it has become very apparent, to both them and me, that they are unprepared for the reality they will face when they walk into a classroom of their own. Use this memoir as an addition to the college coursework so that students will gain a better understanding of the reality that awaits them.

- Which stories from this book illustrate the human side of teaching? How can these stories enhance the existing college curriculum by engaging students and faculty in rich discussions concerning the need to infuse love and compassion into teaching theory?

- The resource section located at the back of this book contains useful materials for helping future teachers learn to lead their classrooms by nurturing positive, caring environments infused with understanding, love, and compassion.

For education policy makers:

- The mantra I recited as an educator was "I teach students, not subjects." This core belief is threaded throughout this memoir. Find the stories of humanity—those stories that illustrate the most important work teachers are doing to help mold and change the lives of students—which can never be measured through standardized testing.

- Teacher attrition is at an all-time high. Which stories in this book highlight educational policies that need to be reformed, ensuring that teachers will stay in the profession, and make the teaching profession appealing to future generations?

- The resources at the back of this book highlight the numerous reasons high-quality teachers are leaving the profession. Use these resources for insight into reforming and designing educational policy that will help reduce teacher attrition rates.

For those seeking personal and professional happiness:

- Locate the stories in the book that most inspire you to continue chasing your dreams of happiness and spiritual fulfillment. Pull snippets of those stories and use them as journal prompts, to help you record and explore your own feelings surrounding personal happiness and purpose.

- It takes courage to make life-altering changes. Which pieces of the book speak most to you about courage? Highlight those pieces and reread often, especially if you begin to feel your courage waver.

- Use the resources in the back of this book to generate ideas about what it means to live a life rooted in purpose and complete happiness. I know the emotional and spiritual pain you feel each day because you know (and dread) what lies ahead. I also know what the other side feels like—a life in which each day is met with absolute excitement and joy! Don't settle—you deserve happiness and fulfillment!

My memoir provides glimpses into the universal principles of love, compassion, hope, and anger that we collectively share as human beings. It is my sincere hope that as you read and interact with these stories, you will discover pieces of you embedded in the words on the pages. And when you do, please pack these newly-discovered pieces of yourself, and carry them with you on your personal and professional journeys to enrich the path you travel with more self-reflection, determination, and purpose.

Teachers Are Not Robots

Lynn, my coworker, is leaving early today for a funeral—her 31-year-old friend was found dead of an alcohol overdose.

It's astounding how many things we keep to ourselves when we are in pain, when we just don't want to deal with the feelings, or are simply emotionally exhausted from retelling the story. I stop by Lynn's room to ask how things are going and to see if she needs help with anything. Tears flow. She has been consumed with guilt over her friend's death, wondering if she had tried hard enough to help her, absolutely devastated she had died entirely too young. The best thing I could do was to let her talk and weep, and then embrace her.

I know Lynn's guilt, pain, sorrow, and loss of hope because I have a brother who has suffered with alcoholism since his mid-twenties. After years on the emotional roller coaster between hope and despair, many friends and family members of alcoholics, like me, are left feeling hopeless and angry, secretly wanting nothing more than to get off that ride. Self-preservation instincts urge them to shut out the offender and protect themselves, rather than staying on the endless, gut-wrenching journey.

I leave Lynn's room with a heavy heart.

One of the most difficult things about teaching is showing up every day, full-throttle, fully energized, ready to engage, entertain, and be at our best.

But teachers are humans with feelings: We are not robots.

We have lives outside the classroom—we have spouses and families; we are grieving over our sick and dying; we are holding on to our hopes and dreams in spite of life's difficulties. And to do our job well, we must shut out all of it—or let it overcome us. On the days it overcomes us, we know our middle-school students will quickly spot our weaknesses. Defensively, we may overcompensate with tighter guidelines and higher expectations, just so we can make it until the final bell rings.

Most of the inner-city students we teach have seen more death, gang violence, and drug and alcohol addiction than all of us combined. To cope, they make jokes and try to laugh it off, masking their feelings of insecurity. But I have never tolerated such behavior. I've worked hard to create an environment where frequent conversations are commonplace and where everyone feels safe, many times sharing tears in heartfelt, engaging, and respectful discussions. I am comfortable showing my human side and demonstrating that strong people also cry and grieve. By embracing this style of teaching, I have built lasting and meaningful relationships with my students.

I head to my classroom to prepare for the day. As homeroom begins, Zea comes to my desk to tell me she is upset. Zea is a tough-around-the-edges girl; it took her until about February to decide she was going to like me. While she deliberated, I was patient, gently asking about her father (who is in and out of prison) and her mother (who completely ignores her). Over these months, I learned Zea is basically raising herself and doing the best she can with the cards she has been dealt. She is an absolutely brilliant writer with a unique voice and an ability to convincingly debate either side of a controversial issue, even when she doesn't believe it herself.

But today, Zea is troubled. She draws really close so only I can hear her and says, "Mrs. Hernandez, I'm upset today." I look up from my desk, welcoming the discussion. This is progress. To my "Why?" she responds,

"Yesterday, we were doing Zumba in my after-school club and the teacher said to the whole group, 'Dance, monkeys, dance!'"

The pen falls out of my hand as I stare at her in disbelief. "Zea, are you absolutely certain that was what the after-school teacher said?" She assures me it was true; she and several of her friends stopped dancing because they were so angry, but in the end, they were told to resume dancing or they would be kicked out of the club.

My next question—which didn't surprise any of my students because we talk openly about racial issues—was, "What color is this teacher?" Zea tells me she is white, and proceeds to say how humiliated and hurt she was by the teacher's comment.

How tragic is this? A student who has been subjected to a degrading racial slur has lost her powerful voice for fear of punishment. I ask Zea if I could share this incident with the class and turn it into a teachable moment. She agrees.

The students are understandably floored, angry, and upset. I use the moment to teach them how to stand up for themselves in a positive, assertive, yet kind way. I give them the words to use so they will be verbally prepared, able to stand strong, and able to keep their personal power in similar situations.

After speaking with Zea later in the day, I learn she doesn't want me to confront the after-school teacher personally, so I make the administration aware of the incident. There is absolutely no excuse for the use of racial slurs and hurtful language.

Perhaps this teacher was raised in ignorance and has never thought about her words and their impact. Regardless of the reasons, she should not be teaching; she is undoing the hard work we are doing build trusting relationships with the students and guide them to become strong, compassionate, effective people who are accepting of others, especially those who appear to be different.

May 2
39 Days Left

Letting Go—Even When It Hurts

As a teacher, there comes a point in your career when you just have to give in and let a few things slide. I learned quickly to let go of my frustration over the constant tapping of pens and pencils. I also learned to let go of the need to be in constant control of my classroom. In fact, by the end of my teaching career, my students were basically running the classroom, very respectfully and efficiently! However, one area I absolutely never gave in on was the Homework Battle.

Today's Homework Battle is brutal. Generally, I don't assign tons of homework, mainly because we accomplish the majority of our work in class. But there are occasional assignments that need to be worked on at home. Last night's homework was to complete an opinion paper on a novel we had just finished.

My first class files in, finds their seats, and I ask them to take out their homework: Out of twenty-four students present, thirteen don't have the assignment done. The Homework Battle continues with my next class: Out of the twenty-nine students present, seven failed to do their homework!

While I have learned through the years not to take it personally, my blood pressure shoots up. I'm sure my face is red. I take a deep breath, walk to the front of the room, and sit on a desk in the lotus position with my legs crossed and my gaze steady. (The students have learned that when this happens, a serious discussion is about to take place—but not before I do a few rounds of deep breathing.) They wait…the silence is deafening. They wait some more, squirming in their seats. (The best part about this whole scenario is I am in complete control, my blood pressure is dropping with each deep breath, and I have disengaged from the battle. This took YEARS to conquer.)

"Class, we have a problem. You were assigned a major writing last night. For those of you who completed it, I thank you. You are placing yourselves well above the competition and proving to yourselves that you are willing to do whatever it takes to succeed—even when you don't want to. That is a sign of true leadership and initiative. But for those of you who actively made a choice not to complete the assignment, you know there are no second chances: You have received a zero."

"But, but, Miss! That's not fair!" they protest.

"No, what is not fair is the way you treat yourselves—continuing to use self-sabotage as a method of coping and default thinking. That will get you nowhere in life. You are almost in ninth grade and must learn that deadlines are real," the admonition I have repeated throughout the school year.

I often wonder if anyone is listening to me. I know the students HEAR me, but do they LISTEN?

This is the end of today's battle…or so I think. At lunchtime, the only "free period" I have today, I call a few parents to inform them their child is missing three or more assignments for the week. Most of the calls go well, but the last call completely floors me.

"Hello Ms. Garrent. I am calling to let you know that Josh is missing three assignments this week and his grade has dropped significantly. I am worried that he may not pass ELA for the quarter, which will put him in jeopardy of failing for the year. I wanted to know if you and I could hatch a plan to keep Josh motivated for the last six weeks of school."

"Mrs. Hernandez, my child will do his homework when he's paid to do his homework. If it's his job, then he should be paid to do it. Quit calling me." With those words, Ms. Garrent hung up on me, and I hung my head in disbelief and defeat.

I stare at the phone, speechless. Am I missing something here? "Paid to do his homework?" What is this world coming to? In fifteen years, I have never had a parent speak to me in that manner or hang up on me. My heart sinks for Josh: If these are the messages he is hearing at home, no wonder he is practically failing all of his classes.

The most difficult time for a teacher—one who cares about and invests in each and every student, and who treats teaching as a profession and a craft—is when he or she has to let go. Sometimes that means letting go of hope and worry. And often, that means completely disconnecting from the deep urge to fix our students' lives so we can make it through another day, month, or year in the classroom.

My lunch hour is over. I had exactly seven minutes to scarf down my food. My next class is coming through the door.

I Teach Students, Not Subjects

I have spent at least a month prepping my students for this day—Career Day is here! Career Day is one of the most significant events at my school. Each spring, teachers and staff prepare, promote, and deliver a vast array of learning opportunities for our students, including as many as twenty-five speakers. Our presenters, who come from various walks of life, give up a day of work to visit our school and speak to the students. We kick off the day with coffee and breakfast for the speakers, and then the entire student body gathers in the auditorium for the keynote speech.

This year's keynote speaker is Jesse A. Saperstein, motivational speaker and author of *Atypical: Life with Asperger's in 20⅓ Chapters*. He tells us about fulfilling his childhood dream of hiking the Appalachian Trail to illustrate the lesson that we often regret the things we don't do. He also speaks candidly about growing up with Asperger's Syndrome and how it excluded him from many social situations and opportunities for friendships, just because he was very different. Society has a hard time with differences, especially in the form of disabilities.

As I look around the auditorium, it is apparent that most of the student body is completely disengaged while the adults are hanging onto Jesse's every word. Several students squirm in their seats, perhaps uncomfortable with the topic, a few sink down into their chairs, several others begin distracting those around them.

Assemblies are a nightmare for teachers if the students have not been properly prepped. It is not a "free period" for teachers when we can let our guards down. In fact, monitoring student behavior in school-wide assemblies puts me on edge, because the students I accompany to such events are a direct reflection on me as a teacher. Thus, I have been preparing my students for Career Day over the past several weeks. We have practiced how to sit up straight and maintain eye contact (even if bored to tears). We have worked diligently on asking meaningful and engaging questions of the individual speakers. Most importantly, we have discussed the value of listening to speakers and fellow classmates so that questions are not repeated (which would indicate that one was not listening).

These topics are not in my curriculum; they are essential life and social skills that eighth-grade students need to know. This is another example of how a teacher's influence extends well beyond the curriculum he or she has been hired to teach.

Thus, a personal mantra I have lived by for fifteen years goes like this: "I teach students, not subjects."

If there is one thing that will make a dramatic improvement in public education, it is for every teacher, administrator, and parent to adopt this seemingly-obvious approach to education because it focuses on preparing our children to succeed in life rather than teaching to a jam-packed curriculum with room only for academic knowledge. Yes, academics are essential, but critical thinking skills, social skills, and life skills bridge the gap between book knowledge and applied knowledge.

Here is what I have witnessed firsthand for many years: When students can't focus on their lessons, it's because other more pressing issues are interfering. Because "I teach students, not subjects" is the mantra I live by, my classroom is a place of love, understanding, and forgiveness. They know the moment one ill word is spoken or any form of disrespect is evident, we will stop the lesson for a discussion about compassion, empathy, and mutual respect for one another.

Taking the time to discuss and teach these important lessons nurtures well-rounded citizens who can leave school at the end of the day with more knowledge, kindness, and understanding for themselves and others.

The Mysteries of Dental Floss
and Menstrual Cycles

A sense of calmness envelopes our building today—the entire seventh-grade class is in upstate New York on a three-day camping trip. Having chaperoned that field trip in the past, I know the great value it has for our concrete-confined urban students. This is the first time many of them will sleep in cabins and walk through the woods. The students will return to campus completely awestruck by all they witnessed in nature.

This year, I volunteered to teach three health classes in addition to my two regular ELA classes, simply because I have observed that our students' health is suffering in many ways, due to a lack of knowledge. Ironically, non-tested courses, such as Health, are being removed from our curriculum every year. It simply amazes me that "the powers that be" consider topics such as nutrition, exercise, sex education, and stress management as non-essential to the education of the whole child.

The health lesson I planned for today revolves around dental health and hygiene. We spend some time talking about brushing. When I say the word "flossing," most of the students look at me like I am speaking in tongues. I stop in mid-sentence when I recognize the shift in energy and focus. After a few minutes of clarifying questions and answers about oral hygiene, it is very apparent the majority of my students has never seen dental floss, wouldn't know what to do with it, or even where to find it in a store. I stop teaching for a moment, jot myself a note to bring dental floss to next week's class, and then continue with the lesson, completely baffled.

In spite of the fact that I interact with my students on such a personal level while teaching—weaving into the curriculum those topics they find interesting and need to know more about—I am still surprised by their willingness to talk with me about almost any conceivable topic.

Shyasia raises her hand to inquire, "Mrs. Hernandez, since we are talking about hygiene, can we talk about our 'friend?'" I know Shyasia is referring to her monthly menstrual cycle and that she, as well as the rest of the class, knows we use proper, scientific terms to describe the characteristics and functions of our bodies.

"Oh, Shyasia, you know the term we use for your 'friend.' Please state it so that all the students, including the boys, can be part of this conversation," I request.

"Our periods—can we talk about that?" she grumbles. Some girls cut their eyes toward Shyasia, noticeably annoyed or uncomfortable with the topic they know we will now discuss. A few boys groan, some sink down in their seats, and the rest look at me for my response.

I nod "Yes."

"Well, what I don't get is why we have them. Why do we get periods anyway?" she asks.

Sometimes I just have to stop and scratch my head in disbelief: Thirty eighth graders are seated in my classroom—many who are sexually active, many who have had their periods for a few years—

but most simply don't know what is happening in their own bodies.

I take a quick poll see if anyone knows why women have periods. The best answer I receive is, "Because there is no baby inside." I take a moment to regroup and gather my thoughts, and then decide, on the spot, to launch into the biology behind the egg, the ovary, and the shedding of the womb's lining.

The entire class is captivated—likely because I am no artist and the fallopian tubes and ovaries I draw on the board resemble an exotic plant, more than parts of a female body. Nevertheless, they are all listening as I explain what happens each month when a sperm cell has not fertilized an egg. The bell for class change will ring soon, so I quickly wrap up the lesson, emphasizing the need for proper hygiene for all parts of the body.

There is something severely wrong with this picture: When I have fourteen-year-old students in my classroom who know nothing about dental floss or menstrual cycles, it's clear they need health education in their school day. A comprehensive health curriculum taught by knowledgeable, trained teachers can help bridge the gap for those students who receive no information, very little information, or misinformation at home. However, administrators continue to expand daily class time for reading and math while taking away health, science, art, and music classes.

Yet, on days like this in Room 719, I know, beyond a shadow of a doubt, that my students are leaving my classroom better able to understand the world inside them and better prepared to live in the world around them.

May 7
36 Days Left

Where's the Appreciation?

It is Day Two of Teacher Appreciation Week, and not a single soul has mentioned it in my school. The students never know and the parents don't seem to realize it either. The administration usually gives a lunch or dessert party, but no one is talking about it this year, not even the teachers.

I survey my teacher friends from around the country on Facebook. Many of them are in Day Two of celebratory activities. Some are receiving a small gift every day this week such as a free planning period, a catered lunch, or a small surprise in their mailbox. Others confirm that they, too, have gone unrecognized.

When I was a young student myself, I would pack up my little gift bag and carry it proudly to my teacher's desk for holidays and Teacher Appreciation Week. My parents knew the value of a good teacher and they made sure my teachers were acknowledged and felt appreciated.

After fifteen years of teaching, I see this forgotten week as a symptom of a bigger issue: Teachers in this country are not valued by society. The teacher's job is seen as less than professional. Many still think we became teachers so we can have our summers off. Summers off? I haven't had a summer off in years. I've been in workshops, moving classrooms, and writing new curriculum for the upcoming school year.

I leave my classroom disheartened by a system and a society that systematically defeats the best efforts of its most essential workers by neglecting the most basic recognition and appreciation.

Every year, in every state across the country, politicians and union reps make decisions that detrimentally affect teachers and the profession on a grand scale. They take away our benefits, freeze our pay, and decide they can no longer compensate us for the advanced degrees we have earned. They also continue to find ways to tie our evaluations to test scores, totally oblivious of the fact that we teachers cannot control when or if students show up in our classrooms regularly, if they have had proper rest and a nutritious breakfast, let alone if they are receptive to learning the content we work so hard to prepare and teach. It simply isn't fair.

The Power of Visuals

Sex! Sex! Sex! I teach eighth graders, and sex is definitely on their minds. So I do what I do best—address the issue full-force, head-on.

Today, a group of girls called me over to tell me about a former student who is now four months pregnant. These girls had been debating whether or not to tell me, as they knew it would break my heart. In the end, they decided I should know. I'm grateful they told me, confirming the love and trust I've worked so hard to build into these relationships each year.

Saddened and distraught, I ride the elevator to my seventh-floor classroom. Pregnant in ninth grade? What kind of life is that for the mother, for the child?

Health class is next. I decide to show a National Geographic documentary titled "Multiples: In the Womb." The students already have sex on the brain, they have just learned their friend is pregnant, and based on the discussion we had on menstrual cycles last week, I'm sure there's still plenty of learning about childbirth that's needed.

We watch the DVD together, pausing to discuss the formation of a fetus when the sperm and egg unite. A few squirm, but all are attentive. The documentary actually tracks the birth of multiple babies and how the babies grow and interact in the womb, so the majority of the film is light-hearted and entertaining.

Then I show the childbirth scene. I don't mute the noises from the delivery room, and I don't fast forward past the crowning of the heads or the passing of the placenta. When I see my students captivated—and completely grossed out—by the natural birth of triplets, I know I have made the right choice to be real, especially when there are television shows such as "Sixteen and Pregnant" that glorify the teenage parenting experience.

The bell rings. No one moves. They are startled. They stare at me. I stare back. It's as if they are paralyzed by fear or, perhaps, disbelief.

I close the lesson with one final recommendation: "Don't have sex until you are ready to birth kids."

They nod, murmur agreement, and silently scuttle out of the room.

May 9
34 Days Left

Betrayed By a Letter

It's Day Four of Teacher Appreciation Week: still no recognition from anyone. I'm trying not to become disheartened about it, but I take my job seriously and it's a real shame that the people responsible for the next generation's education, growth, and progress are some of the most poorly-treated workers in our society.

At 2:37 p.m., three minutes before the end of my final class, the school secretary enters my room and informs me that the assistant principal would like to see me in his office for a few minutes. As instructional time is highly valued in my school and interruptions are not the norm, I am a bit concerned. Has there been some sort of emergency?

I quickly walk to his office. The assistant principal, Philip, and I have a close relationship. He is a true leader who fights for what teachers need, and has been a great friend over the past few years. I walk into his office and can tell immediately by the way the air is hanging, stale and still, that something is wrong. He asks me to sit, hands me a sealed letter, and advises me to open and read it.

My hands are shaking. Philip is white as a sheet. I know that whatever words are lurking on the paper, the news is not good. As I struggle to break the seal, his eyes are downcast. I feel his discomfort. I finally manage to pull the letter out of its envelope, unfold it, and read the first line.

I am under investigation by the New York City Department of Education for misconduct.

I read it again just to make sure I have read it correctly. I look at Philip. He takes a deep breath and informs me that this is a routine procedure and doesn't mean I have done anything wrong.

Really? I am sitting in the assistant principal's office, have been under investigation for God knows how long, and now I have to deal with the legal team? My stomach turns sour and I feel like I might throw up.

I take a deep breath and ask, "Philip, do you know what this is about?" He nods "Yes," but says that neither he nor the principal is allowed to discuss it with me. I'm confused. I don't understand the process. I ask many more questions: "Who is upset with me? What have I done? Am I going to lose my job? Who else knows of this situation?" I'm embarrassed and deeply hurt. I feel like someone has sucked the life out of me. And the worst part is I don't know what I have done and it will be weeks before I find out.

Philip instructs me to call the number on the letter immediately. I will be assigned a legal representative from our union, the United Federation of Teachers, who will help me navigate through the process and provide guidance and support. He also tells me that I am not to discuss this incident with anyone or meet with the case worker without my union representative. The bile rises in my throat.

I get up to leave on wobbly legs and start down the hallway. In a matter of three minutes, my world has been turned upside down and I now must go back into my classroom, put on my smile, and deal with dismissal procedures. My eyes fill with tears and I try to sweep them away before the students see me—but it's too late.

I politely tell them I can't talk about it right now, which confuses them because we always talk about what is bothering us, as that is truly how I teach and live. My truth has been compromised.

So, on Day Four of Teacher Appreciation Week, I have received a letter of misconduct. At least someone has noticed me this year.

May 10
33 Days Left

It Takes Heart and Soul

I spent the majority of last night vacillating between rage and tears. My husband did the best he could to reassure me that the letter was "just a formality," but it did little good. I was filled with anger, fear, and disbelief. I honestly thought the phone call I made yesterday would have answered some of my questions, but once again, my high hopes were crushed by a system that has proven, time and again, how much of a failure it truly is.

After dialing the phone number on the letter, I gave them my case number—pissed off that I had been reduced to a seven-digit number on a crisply-folded piece of paper—and the lady assigned me a union representative and said my hearing date would be Friday, May 24. That was it. She wouldn't tell me what I had done to be under investigation or what I could do to prepare myself. I hung up the phone, my mind clouded by anger, hurt, and uncertainty.

The more I think about the situation, the angrier I become. How can I defend myself if no one is willing to tell me what I have done wrong? Am I going to be thrown to the wolves at my hearing? That does not sit well with me: Where else in America can you be accused of wrongdoing, given a formal letter of misconduct, and be scheduled for a hearing without being told of your offense? Even suspected lawbreakers are told what their alleged crime is before they are arrested.

The best thing about today is that I do not have to go into that school building. A few weeks ago, I scheduled today off to teach a tele-class for my business, The Writing Whisperer. You see, when the new school year started back in September, I knew that the quality of life for public school teachers was not going to get any better. Rather, as local, state, and federal governments all attempt to figure out how public education should be structured and operated, it would get worse.

After fifteen years as a public school teacher, I knew my time was limited due to dealing with issues such as pay freezes, increased insurance rates, principals who forced me to work outside of my contract, and teacher evaluation systems that are neither logical nor fair. While I love teaching, I refuse to be someone's whipping girl or stay in a job where my value is not recognized or appreciated.

So last fall, I hatched a business plan and partnered with a business coach, an accountant, a virtual assistant, and a website designer. A few months later, I officially launched The Writing Whisperer. Since the start of my business, I've worked eighteen to twenty-hour days, giving heart and soul to my students for the first ten hours of my day, then coming home and pouring what's left of me into my future for the last ten hours. Most nights I fall into bed, completely exhausted by all that is required of me, yet so content, knowing my hard work is paying off. I am creating a future where I can call the shots, pee when I want to pee, and be treated like a respectable human being, not a number on a piece of paper in a school system that continues to fail on so many levels.

May 13
32 Days Left

The Effect of Stress

Bruce, the principal, is back from the camping trip. I stop by to request we have a chat about the letter. I have decided that I will NOT be thrown to the wolves—I don't care if that is the protocol or not. He tells me he will stop by to talk during one of my planning periods.

I have a migraine. This is not surprising, considering that during the past few days, including the weekend, I have been racking my brain to figure out what in the hell I might have done to be investigated for misconduct. I have been teaching about the Holocaust through the book *Night* by Elie Wiesel, so maybe an upset student went home and shared his or her feelings with parents? It's completely plausible and possible. Or maybe someone reported me for using the student restroom one day, because I was sick and couldn't make it to the eighth floor during my three-minute break between classes? Or maybe a colleague is upset with me for something I said?

It's very clear to me that because I have been told nothing, I am freaking out and my imagination is going crazy trying to make sense of it all. It's affecting every aspect of my life—sleeping, eating, and working. Not knowing may be the worst part of it all.

When I let my students know I am not feeling well, they really are angels. They know how to respect someone who respects them. For that I am so grateful, especially on days when my head explodes at the clatter of a pen hitting the floor.

We spend some time reading and discussing *Night*. As I teach the lesson, I realize paranoia has definitely set in: I wonder if I'm being baited, if a student is collecting data for this investigation, or if my words will be used against me later. I tell myself I must stop these irrational thoughts, as they are making me someone whom I have never been—a skeptical, angry, insecure teacher.

At last, the teaching day ends. Bruce arrives and sits down next to me at my desk.

"Bruce, I know you can't talk about the letter, legally, but I'm not walking into that investigation blind and unable to defend myself. So I ask that you give me something to go off of here."

"Shannon, this letter is for an incident that occurred LAST May," he states.

My mind screeches to a halt. Last May? I can't remember what I did last month, let alone twelve months ago.

"Last May? What the hell, Bruce? And you still can't talk about it with me?" I implore.

Bruce tells me that a parent filed the complaint against me last May. He won't say what the complaint was, but does say similar complaints have been filed in the past and things turned out fine for all teachers involved.

I am furious. I start pacing around the room, realizing just how dysfunctional this school system really is. My principal has known since last May about the complaint? And what honest person takes twelve months to conduct a private investigation without letting the offender know what is happening?

I stop dead in the middle of my classroom when a thought slaps me upside the head: What I have done must not be THAT bad, because I have been teaching this whole year and nothing has been said, I haven't been removed from my classroom, and no one has mentioned anything to me.

I take a deep breath and let out a sigh of relief.

May 14
31 Days Left

Epiphany

Sometimes it takes a teacher a little while to figure out what's going on in the classroom, to sense the overall vibe and identify who is responsible for the group's ebb and flow. The past three days have been glorious! The classroom tone is calm and the students are cool and collected—because Myron has been absent.

Myron and I have had several rough patches this year. He doesn't respond to open kindness because he is suspicious of ulterior motives; it's a trust issue. I learned rather quickly to choose my words wisely when talking with him. Myron also doesn't respond well to raised voices. He clams up and shuts down because it reminds him of his awful home life with a mother who is invisible, unless she needs to scream about something that is upsetting her, which is most of the time.

However, Myron does respond well to sarcastic humor. I realized this about a month ago when I was fed up with his attitude, fed up with his lack of effort, and fed up with him never completing his homework. Basically, he was taking up space in my classroom, and that doesn't fly with me. Students must actively contribute to the overall positive learning environment we have worked hard to create. Otherwise, they gotta go!

"Myron, what do you want to do with your life?" I asked him privately.

"I don't know. I just really want to play video games and ride my bike," he replied, snidely.

"But Myron, that's not gonna make your wife happy. Do you want kids one day?" I continued.

"Of course I want kids, Mrs. Hernandez. Who doesn't want kids?"

"So, let me get this straight: If you GET to high school, you are going to most likely drop out, based on the effort I see right now. Then, you are going to start a family. And when it's time for parent-teacher meetings, you are going to roll on up to your child's school on your bike with your joystick in hand? This is how you want your kids to know you as a father?" I questioned, sternly.

He looked at me, smiled, grasped the vision, and said, "That's crazy. Can you imagine me doing that?"

To which I exclaimed, with a big, enthusiastic, sarcastic voice, "Yes! That's what is so sad about this whole conversation! I can really, really see you pulling into your child's school on your bike with your joystick!"

And that was all it took to get him to lose the attitude. We have had some setbacks and successes since that conversation, but overall, Myron has improved his behavior, participated more in class, and completed more homework.

I learned something important about myself as a teacher that day: I refuse to give up on my students, even the ones who are enigmas to me and get under my skin the most. In fact, I learned something even more important through this exchange: Every student is reachable, even those who possess a tough exterior or who show up only once a week.

Teachers should work hard to ensure each student feels valued, loved, understood, and safe at school, regardless of the other "things" going on in their lives.

May 15
30 Days Left

What Teachers REALLY Want

It's a special day today! Our literacy coach has arranged for the English Language Arts team to meet at the local Barnes & Noble bookstore and map out curriculum for next year. We have been going through some changes in the department and in the approaches we use for teaching our student population, so there is much work to do! We choose the Barnes & Noble on 86th Street in Manhattan because it has a large table in the back, a friendly, warm environment conducive to collaboration, and teaching resources and children's literature right at our fingertips.

Our workday begins and we are fresh and bright with several innovative ideas for jazzing up the curriculum. We spend this important time in deep discussions, brainstorming ways we can teach content to meet our students' needs, and staying laser-focused for the entire morning. When we realize lunchtime has arrived, we head out to the local diner.

BLISS. Do you know what it's like to be a teacher and actually get to EAT, rather than gulp down food? Do know what it's like to be able to sit with another adult and engage in intelligent conversation over lunch? Like I said, BLISS! After our wonderful lunch, we head back to our worktable, grab a cup of coffee, and work through the afternoon. This may be one of the most enjoyable and productive staff development days I've had in my teaching career.

Later that evening, I reflect on this beautiful day and journal about what truly makes a positive impact on me as a teacher:

What Teachers REALLY Want

- Teachers want to be heard: More often than not, the top-down education system has robbed us of our voices. Teachers want to be seen as essential to fixing the broken system we now have and in shaping a new education system.

- Teachers want to be able to actually eat—not inhale—their lunches. Being able to eat with other adults would be icing on the cake!

- Teachers need to interact with other adults in collaborative and supportive environments, because we plan higher-quality lessons when we are able to bounce our ideas off each other. All too often, we are closed off in our classrooms, dealing with the pressures that come with teaching by ourselves. (And for the record, high-pressure meetings do not count as adult interaction.)

- Teachers want to become better teachers, but attending the same tired workshop year after year doesn't cut it. We know what our development needs are, and want to choose the meetings and workshops that will increase our capabilities.

- Teachers want and need two full planning periods every day. We don't want to sacrifice that essential time to cover classes for which the administration can't or won't hire a substitute. Working back-to-back class periods all day long is not sustainable, and causes us to be less than our best for the students.

- Teachers want the school to pay for classroom materials. Many teachers in this city have to spend their own money at copy centers so they have worksheets for class: This is unconscionable! We shouldn't have to buy our own tissues, pencils, or notebook paper either. (My school supplies me with one box of tissue each month. We run short, of course. I don't even want to think about how much of my own money I spend on tissue for my classroom.)
- Teachers want to be able to pee when we need to pee. Yes, I said pee. Every single day, teachers are denied the time for this most basic body function. What other business robs its professionals of bathroom breaks?
- Teachers want coffee, and they are willing to pay for it. I don't know how many times over the years I have suggested reasonable ways to make this happen, but the idea has been shot down every time!
- If you scan this list again, it's quite clear and simple: Teachers want to be treated like humans—humans who are heard, nurtured, and respected. Honestly, is that too much to ask? Somehow, somewhere along the way we lost sight of the "human" in education.
- Teachers aren't lobbying for bigger classrooms—we're managing in the spaces we are given. (You will often find us teaching in hallways, lunchrooms, and closets!) We aren't complaining about our pay, because we didn't go into teaching for the money (GASP!). What we are asking for are simple fixes.

Politicians, both federal and state, are asked what they desire in education. Unions are asked what they want for education. Administrators, parents, and students are asked what they want for education.

But NO ONE has asked the teachers what they want.

We teachers—who know the difficulties, problems, and opportunities in education far better than the other stakeholders—are forced to take what is dished out without having our say. I do not understand why the most important people in the educational system—we who are educating future generations and shaping the future of our nation—are not given a place at the table!

May 16
29 Days Left

A Pocket Full of Dreams

I show up at school this morning feeling refreshed and energized after yesterday's wonderful Barnes & Noble workday with my colleagues. I am wearing a blue and white floral dress with a belt and a pair of straw wedges, and my hair has been styled into a sleek, blonde bob. My students definitely know something is amiss, as I am most comfortable in khakis, flip flops, and a blouse of some sort—not too plain, not too frilly.

Zea is completely flabbergasted by my outfit. She can't seem to believe that I even OWN a dress, let alone am wearing one, and she is totally loving the shoes. She calls me over to her desk for a word with me.

"Mrs. Hernandez, you wear dresses?" she asks in disbelief.

"Why yes, yes I do Zea. I have lots of dresses that I wear, mainly in the summer. The temperature has to be just right and I have to be feeling great."

"Well, I need to tell you something," she continues. I wait. I love Zea—you just never know what she is going to say next. (The best part is I have taught her that she can say pretty much anything she wants to, but she has to watch her tone and word choices so that what she says is not misinterpreted by others.) I watch the cogs spin in her mind as she looks for the right words and forms the sentences she wants to eventually speak.

"You look like a white housewife! You know, the ones, those ones from TV!" she exclaims, "The real pretty ones in the flower dresses." I can't do anything but smile—she has made my day.

"I am a white housewife," I tell her.

"I know, Mrs. Hernandez, and you look like one today!"

I get the class organized and we delve into the lesson. Every teacher's end-of-the-school year challenges are, first, making it to the final bell of the school year happily, and second, keeping our students super-busy. The cards are stacked against us—the weather is gorgeous and everyone is restless, wanting nothing more than to be outside in the bright sunshine. The students are excited to be moving on to high school and have mentally checked out of anything related to academics. At the same time, teachers are exhausted from the many extra tasks needing attention to close out the school year properly, plus the plethora of field trips, dances, and school activities that are taking their toll on our energy levels and psyches.

In today's lesson, I'm trying something new which I hope will be a huge hit. I begin by playing "Empire State of Mind," a song by Alicia Keys, which immediately captures the class's full attention. We talk about the lyrics and what it means to have a "pocket full of dreams." When I am sure the students understand why dreams in life are important, we move forward with the lesson.

Everyone takes out a piece of paper. They are given three minutes to write down all the dreams they have for their futures: high school, college, traveling, their dream houses and families, dining at special restaurants, etc. They look so eager and excited. I set the timer and tell them to begin making their lists.

I watch from the front of the room for a minute. Some students are writing fast and furiously; they have numerous ideas freely flowing from their minds onto the paper. But other students are stuck; they get to number three or four on their list and don't have anything else to write. I know this shouldn't upset me, as I've conducted this lesson before, but it does. It also makes me incredibly sad, because the students who have stopped writing have also stopped dreaming—and they are the ones who are so burdened and troubled in life.

The timer buzzes. I ask a few students to share their ideas (if they are comfortable) and many hands shoot into the air. All listen attentively as we hear dreams being read aloud:

- Conquer a video game I've been playing for years
- Become a professional basketball player
- Learn to dance ballet
- Move away from this city to somewhere quiet
- Make my mom proud
- Help my dad stay out of prison
- Travel to China
- Find a cure for cancer
- Convince my family to eat better and exercise more
- Become a doctor

The room is silent. These eighth-grade students—in this loving and trusting classroom we have worked so hard to build—are sharing aloud their souls and deepest desires with one another. No one is ridiculing anyone, and no one is vying for attention.

It's just pure dream-sharing.

And then, something even more beautiful happens: The students who had stopped writing have been inspired by listening to their classmates, and now, they are adding to their personal dream lists, too.

I instruct the students to continue to listen, brainstorm, and discuss their dreams in groups of four. While I move around the room and listen to the conversations, a thought hits me hard: Has anyone else ever asked these students about their hopes and dreams for their futures? I stop the class and ask that question. Very few students say, "Yes." In fact, most say they have never really thought about it before.

In this moment of my teaching career, I realize we are so busy teaching a curriculum that is so scripted, test-heavy, and inauthentic that we have lost the opportunity to connect with students on a personal level. Instead, we are focused on raising test scores and teaching testing strategies, day in and day out. Teachers, too, have forgotten what it's like to create inspiring lessons, to have heart-to-heart conversations, and to facilitate projects that help the students grow as humans.

The bell is about to ring, but a magnificent thing has happened today in Room 719: My students are leaving the classroom inspired, thinking about their futures, with personal dreams on their minds. And I am excited because the next class is coming through the door and I have the opportunity to teach this magical lesson all over again.

May 17
28 Days Left

The Lives They Live

We have continued our reading of *Night* by Elie Wiesel. It is not an easy book to digest, but the students can relate to many aspects of the author's struggle to survive the Holocaust concentration camps. They feel his pain when he is imprisoned and beaten for not doing what the power-hungry officers ordered him to do. They relate to his severe hunger and starvation and lack of personal attention. While I am in no way implying that my students have lives as horrific as those in the concentration camp, many face struggles similar in type, if not in intensity.

As I look over my classroom, I know the personal stories and histories of most of the students who are entrusting me with their futures. One young man in my class is scared to death of walking out the front door of his building: There are days he refuses to leave his house and come to school for fear of being taunted and beaten by the local gangs who have targeted him as a weak, shy boy. He is an emotional wreck. Most days, he sleeps during my class, because our classroom is a safe space where he can let his guard down and get the rest his body and mind crave.

Just last week, a young lady confided to me that she is being forced by her mother to paint her stepfather's toenails every night. When I asked a few clarifying questions to understand better what was really going on, she shut down and cried. And because she refused to comply last week, her cell phone was taken away.

I've been sharing my lunch with one of the young ladies who remains in the classroom during lunch and recess. She eats her cafeteria lunch during the day and then takes home what I bring her so she has something to eat at night. Her mom never seems to get around to cooking dinner for her and her five siblings.

My heart breaks for the young man who wants nothing more than to be noticed by his mother. He tells me that when he comes home from school, his mother is dressed in "nice clothing." She hands him a ten dollar bill to cover his after-school snack and dinner, leaves around 5:00, and returns well after he has finally fallen asleep on the couch that serves as his bed. He cries when we do get the chance to discuss it—always in private and usually at lunchtime—because he feels so emotionally drained and disconnected from his mother.

These are the stories of just four of the seventy-seven students I am responsible for this year. They wear the armor of anger, fear, and pain every day, so forgiveness doesn't come easily for them. Consequently, a common thread woven through many of our discussions, both group and one-on-one, is forgiving those who have hurt us.

Today's class begins with a low-key conversation about how Elie Weisel rose above his pain and humiliation to forgive the people who treated him so inhumanely throughout his imprisonment.

"Mrs. Hernandez, that's whack. You're saying Elie forgave those people for what they did? How is that possible?"

"I would have killed them," says a vocal boy from the back row.

"Yeah, I agree with you. You can't forgive people like that. You can't forgive or forget," agrees a young lady seated to my right.

I allow these free-flowing discussions because my students must have a place where they can voice their thoughts and feelings. After a few minutes, I move the topic closer to home turf: How can we forgive those people in our lives who have caused us pain? The students explode into discussions at their tables. I travel around the room, hearing a few stories of forgiveness and many stories of continuing grudges against aggressors. Forgiveness is not easy, but it is needed in order to heal and move on with life.

Of course, the bell is about to ring at this pivotal point in our rich discussion. I wrap up by assigning homework, asking the students to write about a time they forgave someone or about a person they want to forgive, but haven't been able to yet.

The bell rings and they file out. I know this lesson has made an impression because they continue their conversations down the hallway and into the science room. Now, I must figure out how I will teach them about forgiveness by this time next Monday. I am thankful to have the weekend to plan my next moves.

May 20
27 Days Left

Lessons in Forgiveness

I spend the weekend trying to figure out where, exactly, I wanted to go with this forgiveness lesson. It appears that I have two "camps"—those who forgive willingly and those who want nothing at all to do with forgiveness.

As my students file in, they take out their journals and lay them on their desks. Something amazing has happened: EVERY SINGLE STUDENT completed the written homework over the weekend. I've been teaching long enough to know this means they are fully invested in the topic and ready to make huge academic progress today.

I begin class by asking the students to share their journal entries with one another. As I walk around the room and listen, I realize how profound their writing has become. A year's worth of teaching about the importance of word choice and how it affects tone has definitely paid off. Each student has thought about the structure of his or her piece, the message he or she wanted to convey, and the overall tone of the piece. And not only are they sharing their work, they are reflecting on these very writing principles as they discuss and analyze their own writings.

As a veteran teacher, I have learned to "let go" and allow lessons to evolve organically, based on student needs and interests. This method of teaching took me about twelve years to master and it has transformed my classroom in profound and positive ways.

So today, I am throwing out the lesson plan I labored over this weekend, and am going with the flow of student energy and interest.

Standing at the front of the room, a new idea comes to me: This is a perfect opportunity to teach the students how to identify the most compelling sentences in their work that highlight their feelings on forgiveness. After giving them some examples and modeling the procedure, I give the class time to work.

By the end of the lesson, the students have created beautifully-colored index cards, each with a stirring, personal quote about forgiveness:

"Forgiveness does more than cover the wound."
"Forgiving a person is not as easy as it seems."
"Forgiving, but not forgetting, can make you feel like a free human being."
"Forgiveness makes you realize how irrelevant your anger was."
"Not everything is worth forgiving."
"It takes toughness and a shift in pride to forgive."
"Forgiveness heals the heart."
"Sometimes it's not about always being right."
"Forgiveness is not for the person that inflicted your pain; it is for your own healing and the ability to move on."

We decide to construct a bulletin board display in the hallway so my students can share their thoughts on forgiveness with the rest of the school. The bulletin board is brightly colored with pure emotion and the wonder of words.

I take a look at the wisdom of my students and realize that I, too, have much work to do in the area of forgiveness.

One of the greatest rewards of teaching is the lessons I learn from my students.

May 21
26 Days Left

Tears Over Fruit and Cookies

The fruit and cookie platter arrived at 10:00 this morning in recognition of Teacher Appreciation Week, which was two weeks ago. I don't want to sound ungrateful, but I was teaching all morning and by lunchtime, most of the food was gone. It made me sad on so many levels.

I'm not sure what gesture would properly recognize Teacher Appreciation Week, but fruit and cookies arriving days late doesn't cut the mustard. I realize school budgets are tight, but sometimes, the things we desire most as teachers don't cost any money at all.

More About What Teachers Want

- Duty-free lunch every day.
- Not to have to sit with kids on detention during my lunch.
- An extra free period as a token of appreciation.
- A "thank you" once in a while for the hard work we do every day for the students.
- Productive meetings, not a rehash of what's already been said and discussed in prior sessions.
- The opportunity to lead a staff workshop to share my expertise.
- To introduce a new program or idea without being shut down immediately and told, "That won't work."

You see, Teacher Appreciation Week shouldn't be about spending money on teachers or buying an obligatory platter of food once a year. Rather, it should be an ongoing, conscientious effort to treat teachers with respect and admiration, in an effort to build their morale and encourage them to stay positive about their chosen profession.

May 22
25 Days Left

A Visitor in Room 719

Something crazy happens today. From the front of the classroom, all is quiet and going well. The students are engaged in the lesson and I can see their cogs turning while they process our class discussion. All of a sudden, out of nowhere, Levon screams, jumps up, grabs his backpack off the floor, and runs to the back of the room. Instinctively, other students also scream, bolt out of their seats, and take off in various directions. Before I know it, some of my eighth graders are out in the hallway, peeking through a crack in the door, trying to figure out what is going on. A few are perched on the tables.

I realize then what has happened: This is a city child's reaction to a bug or mouse scurrying across the floor. I've seen this before and know what to do this time.

I instruct everyone in the room to take a deep breath. I allow the kids in the hallway to stay there for the time being, where they feel safe. (Why move them back into the classroom? I have enough to deal with!) I ask everyone to pick up their bags and put them on the tables: If I can clear the floor, this process will go much smoother and faster. Then I instruct everyone to curl their legs into their bodies and rest their feet on their chairs. We all take a few more deep breaths together.

"Levon, what happened?" I ask as I walk towards him. He is standing on a chair at this point.

I'm trying not to die of laughter, managing to remain professional and caring.

"A huge-ass bug just walked across my shoe! It violated me!" he screams. The class bursts into giggles—they're not laughing at him, but with him. Most of them would have reacted the same way.

"Where did it go, Levon, which direction?"

He points toward the wall on the left, so I walk over to investigate. I finally see it—a gigantic water bug, about three inches in length, with a crunchy outer shell and spindly legs. It's black and blends in perfectly with the linoleum floors.

I simply say, "Oh yes. That, my friend, is a water bug."

But my students react as if I had said, "It's a Tyrannosaurus Rex!" because the three closest boys jump up and freak out. Two take off across the room. Jason makes a quick escape to a nearby chair and throws his pencil at the bug, causing it to scurry closer to a group of girls. They freak out, curl up tighter, squeeze their eyes shut, and moan loudly.

"Jason, that wasn't a bright idea. Please don't throw objects at living things," I remind.

The bug is moving closer to Matt, who springs out of his seat and tries to stab it with a chair leg. As you can imagine, this doesn't work either, and now the bug is on the move. I am trying to close in on the water bug myself, but every time I get near it, I hear a squeal from across the room or another student makes a clean getaway into the hall. I make a quick assessment: Five students are in the hallway, seven are perched on tables or chairs, and the rest are curled tightly into little balls.

Then, out of nowhere, Valerie stomps across the room, voice booming, "What's wrong with you boys? Step on it!" And in a matter of twenty seconds, she has followed the bug's trail, moved a bookcase, and stomped it dead. The class erupts into applause, lauding Valerie as the hero who saved everyone in Room 719.

I check the clock. The bell will ring in five minutes, too late to continue with today's lesson. I get everyone back into their seats and try to explain that we have nothing to fear from bugs and mice because we're so much larger and to try to remember that for the next time. I know my attempt is falling on deaf ears, as city kids have a difficult time coping with nature in general. I took them on a picnic to the park once...but that's a story for another time.

May 23
24 Days Left

Safety in Words and Paper Flowers

One of my students has been quite withdrawn lately. I have stopped to check on her a few times in other classrooms, at lunch, and at different points throughout her school day. Those moments confirm there is definitely something going on that's out of her norm.

During today's independent reading time, Dee refused to read. Dee is usually an avid reader who consumes two to three novels a week. She will take any book I recommend and give it a test read. (The good news is she likes most of what I have handed her.) She read *The Color Purple* earlier in the year, connecting with Celie on such a deep level that it caused me to pause and take note of what may be going on in her life.

Today, Dee is choosing to write in her journal instead of reading. While this is fine with me, the school would frown upon a student choosing to write rather than read during the twenty-five minute reading block which is required in each of my classes every day. There was a time when I would not have allowed this, but now I know better. If the child wants to write, I'm going to let her write.

As the class is getting ready to move into the lesson, I see Dee stroll toward the pencil sharpener near my desk. She hesitates for a moment and then drops a folded piece of paper onto my lesson plan book. I pretend I don't see it and continue teaching.

After class ends, I wish the students a pleasant day and walk back to my desk. I open the piece of paper and read:

Dear Mrs. Hernandez,
I am starving. I haven't had dinner or breakfast. I was
punished again for speaking my mind and standing up
for myself. I'm sorry I can't focus. I'll keep trying.

Love, Dee

My heart goes out to this girl. I know Dee's story: She was placed in foster care with a foster mother who is rash, judgmental, and cruel. Dee must walk the thinnest line each and every day, not saying or doing even one small thing to upset her foster mom lest she be punished with the removal of food.

I walk down the hall to the art room where the staff refrigerator is located. I grab my lunch, head back toward the math classroom, pop in next to Dee's desk, whisper for her to come and visit me for a moment, then head back to my classroom. I spread out a few napkins for a makeshift tablecloth, empty my lunch bag, and make a centerpiece of paper flowers out of tissue paper and a twist tie. We sit down to share a meal together.

I give her my orange, peeled and segmented, my roasted almonds, and my cherry yogurt. And we dine. In that moment, Dee knows she is loved and valued beyond belief. She is being nourished in body and spirit, and I see a complete transformation in her. She looks at me from across our intimate table and says that she has never had a tablecloth or flowers during a meal. And then she cries, relieved she has found a teacher who is also a friend.

Judgment Day

For the past two weeks, I have been sick to my stomach over the misconduct investigation. I can't eat. Last night I didn't sleep. Today is the day I travel into downtown Brooklyn for my misconduct hearing.

I arrive at 10:45 a.m. and meet Linda, my union representative. She welcomes me with a smile, and I burst into tears. She sits next to me in the waiting room, completely sympathetic, and hands me a tissue. We spend a few minutes trying to pull me together before we are called back into the cold cubicle with the bare walls and icy white paint.

As we are guided to the round table in the cubicle, Linda gives me a few instructions:

- If you need to speak to me alone, request that and the investigator will leave.
- Whisper if we are speaking privately, because the walls are paper-thin.
- If you don't remember the allegation from a year ago, simply state that you don't remember.
- Let me do the talking. Answer questions with a simple yes or no.

As simple as these instructions seem, they make my stomach lurch. I feel like a criminal. My body goes clammy and I focus solely on staying upright, catching my breath, and staying alert.

The investigator strides into the tiny room and takes a seat, looking pleasant enough. She has long red hair and a kind smile. She sits across from us at the round table, opens the folder, and begins.

"Ms. Hernandez, you are here because of a report we received from your principal dated April 26, 2012," she states.

My heart stops. WHAT? Did I hear her correctly? My principal reported me? He said that it was a parent who reported me. I grip the chair tightly, steadying myself.

"On the morning of April 26, 2012, your principal witnessed you inappropriately touching a group of girls in Room 719. He states that he walked into the classroom where several of you were in a circle, embracing in a hug." The investigator looks up and her gaze meets mine.

In that moment, several things happened, although I'm not sure which one happened first. I remember just staring blankly at the investigator's long red hair. Her face seemed tired and her eyes caring. I wondered if she liked her job. I remember looking at my union representative. She was looking at me and I just shook my head slowly. I know that I had been instructed not to talk, but I make a choice to break the silence.

"I'm sorry, but you brought me here for a group hug that happened over a year ago?" I ask, in total disbelief. "That's what this investigation is about?" My tone was sharp and not at all how I usually speak.

She nods her head slowly and picks her eyes up off the report to meet mine again.

"I've been emotionally and physically sick for two weeks over a group hug that happened a year ago? My principal reported this?"

My voice is shaking in anger and disbelief and I know I shouldn't be speaking, but no one stops me. The investigator looks to my representative. Linda asks her to leave and when we are alone, inquires about the details of the incident.

I remember like it was yesterday—April 26, 2012 was a special day. I had finished administering the high-stakes eighth-grade ELA state exam to my wonderful group of special education students. They had finished the test, so proud they hadn't run out of time and completely ecstatic because they were well-prepared to write the essay. They were so proud of the work they had just completed and had struggled with all year long. At the end of the test and after all the materials had been collected, one of my students said, "Can we have a group hug? We did awesome!"

And so we embraced—there were about seven of us in the huddle. I gave them a pep talk about hard work and we circled up, much like a sports team does when strategizing. In that moment—I remember it clearly—the principal walked through the door. He smiled, did what he had come to do, and left.

Linda looks at me and shakes her head in disbelief that we are even discussing this allegation. She calls the investigator back into the cubicle. I let Linda do the talking at this point. I get lost in her words because my mind is cloudy and my heart is heavy.

At one point, Linda recaps the story to the investigator and points out that I shouldn't be sitting here for an alleged hug, especially when there are sexual offenders still sitting in classrooms across the city.

I remember her stating that this hearing is a complete waste of time.

I know I shouldn't say any more but I have one burning question. I sit up straight, and I look at the investigator head-on.

"Why has it taken you so long to investigate this case?" I ask. I assume there are thousands of other bogus cases clogging this screwed-up system, but I want to hear her answer.

She tells me that for the last year, she has been chasing my former students—now spread across the five boroughs and preparing for the end of their freshman year of high school—to obtain their statements. She has visited their schools, their houses, and their cousins' houses. And with the next piece of information she shares with me, I know that everything I have ever stood for, as a human being and a public school teacher, matters.

"And Ms. Hernandez, not one student or their family would speak against you. Time and again, each one said, "'Leave her alone. She's the best teacher I ever had.'"

I weep tears of relief, gratitude, and joy. My anxiety is gone, and the shame has dissolved.

The investigator tells me the case will be closed because the allegation was unfounded. She looks tired and downtrodden. I want to ask her if she feels fulfilled in her job, but in that moment, I don't really care.

Linda and I are dismissed and we take a seat in the lobby. I am still sobbing tears of relief. While I know this could be the end of the saga, I decide I'm not going to let it be. This is adult bullying at its best and I won't stand for it.

As I sit on the sofa in the lobby, one thing becomes very clear to me: My decision to leave this profession has not been a mistake or a miscalculation on my part. It has been considered from all angles.

Since I am tenured and leaving at the end of June, I have nothing to lose: My principal will know exactly how I feel about him within the week.

The train ride back to the school ends too quickly. I don't want to enter the building. I don't want to see my principal yet because I'm livid. I need a few days to calm down and collect my thoughts before I request that meeting with him.

I float through the rest of the afternoon somewhere between clouded thoughts of rage, disappointment, and astonishment. How could my principal, who I respected completely, throw me under the bus? I have done nothing but give my heart and soul to this school for the past four years. I recognize that my heart hurts so much right now because what I thought was true simply wasn't.

It's the Friday before Memorial Day and I am grateful to have a three-day weekend to calm down and heal so I can finish the last four weeks of this career with dignity. I pack up my students for dismissal and lead them down the seven flights of stairs to the back door of the school. Bruce is waiting on the sidewalk.

"Hey, Shannon, I wanted to see how your hearing turned out. Do you have time to talk?" he asks.

I can't believe my ears. Mid-stride, I come to a dead stop and inhale so deeply that I feel the air completely fill my lungs and my jacket slip off my chest. Outside of the school, on a public sidewalk, in my current emotional state is not where I want to have this conversation.

I turn on my heel, stopping three feet short of his face.

"Bruce, I'm not talking about this right now. I have nothing to say to you," I state in a strained tone.

I've never felt more powerful than I do at this moment. I know that I have tenure, I know my rating at the end of the year is going to be flawless, and I also know that I am not coming back to work in this failing system. A wave of enlightenment washes over me and in that moment, I know that I can pretty much say anything I want—yet I hold my tongue. I will not "air my laundry" in public.

Bruce looks at me as if he is deeply hurt or taken aback by my brashness.

"Can I give you a call this weekend to check in?" he asks.

I take one step forward, raise my finger in his face, and proclaim, "My time to report back to this job, as stated in my contract, begins at 8:10 on Tuesday morning. Do not call me this weekend. If you want to talk to me, you can find me on Tuesday."

And then, I turn briskly on my heel and walk away. I have just stood up to a silent bully—my boss.

May 28
22 Days Left

The Case for Outlawing Makeup

As sick as I am of twenty-minute lunches (or less), I am equally sick of staff members who want to outlaw every single thing students do to express themselves.

My school adheres to a strict uniform policy. Every student shows up in navy blue pants, dress, or skirt and a light blue polo shirt with a collar. Socks must be either navy blue or white and absolutely no jewelry is allowed, except for watches and earrings. This year, we added bright hair accessories to the cannot-wear list.

I understand why the cannot-wear list is so exhaustive: Each time a student devises a new way to express their uniqueness, a new item is added to the uniform policy.

While sitting at a grade-level meeting today, one of the teachers suggested we ban the wearing of makeup. I about fell out of my chair. Her position is that the application of lipstick and makeup during class is too disruptive. It is the end of the year, and I have limited energy reserves to deal with such foolishness. Outlaw makeup? No way! I must speak up on this one.

As I state all the reasons for allowing the girls to continue wearing makeup, the biggest one emerges: If we want our students to know how to represent themselves in public—including wearing colors that complement their skin tones—then why don't we sit with them and actually have a conversation, rather than banning makeup entirely?

Just last week, I spoke with one of my eighth graders about how harsh she looked in her bright orange-red lipstick. It was a very cordial, candid conversation, and guess what? The next day, she showed up wearing a much lighter shade. I complimented her, and she smiled and glowed the rest of the day. It was a beautiful lesson, one rooted in affectionate concern about the student's success in life.

Naturally, students this age experiment with different ways to express themselves. But because most parents leave for work well before their children leave for school, they are not able to guide their child's clothing, accessory, or makeup choices. Thus, if we ban every attempt at self-expression with our all-inclusive uniform policy, our students will have very few opportunities to learn what is and isn't proper for various social situations, and we teachers will have very few opportunities to help them.

May 29
21 Days Left

Standing in My Truth

Yesterday, the principal paid me a visit. I wasn't sure I could speak civilly to him. He betrayed me, he lied about me, and he made me out to be something and someone I am not. As he entered the room, I remained seated at my desk. I wasn't going to make an inviting gesture in any way, shape, or form. He chose to pull up a chair on the other side of my desk. I said nothing.

"I'm sorry, Shannon. I made a poor judgment last year," he stated.

"Poor judgment? That's what you call it, Bruce? You reported me to your legal team for sexual misconduct. Do you have any idea what that means? It means that if I had been found guilty, I'd be registered as a sex offender. My life would be over—because of a group hug. Bruce, do you hear yourself?"

I am trying to remain calm, but the tears are welling up in my eyes, my voice is starting to shake, and my limbs are trembling. I get up and walk around the room in an effort to release some energy.

Bruce tries to apologize several more times, but this is the one time in my life I have decided I can't forgive. I can't forgive someone who betrayed me in this manner. I can't forgive him for almost ruining my life. And I can't forgive him for keeping this secret for over a year while there was a team of people investigating me. I can't forgive him for being such an unprofessional and uncaring leader. But above all, I won't forgive him for trying to make me look like a bad, misguided teacher after giving my heart and soul to this school, these children, and to my colleagues.

I tell him all of this. And once I start, the rage doesn't stop. I tell him I won't come back to be the science literacy coordinator part-time next year. I tell him he doesn't deserve to have hard-working, honest, loving teachers under his "guidance." I tell him he's a coward and that if he didn't want me to hug students or if he perceived it as a problem, he should have come to me to discuss his concerns.

Then I tell him he has earned one thing from me: At least two chapters in my book.

At that, he goes silent and looks at me, his eyes welling up with tears. My heartstrings are pulled a little in the direction of forgiveness, but I'm too irate. I tell him that my case was ruled unfounded because not one student or parent confirmed that I was out of line by handing out an innocent hug. And I tell him that he is what is wrong with the educational system.

Then, I ask him how many hugs he thinks our students get on a daily basis? He doesn't answer. Finally, I tell him, in a voice filled with disgust, I will continue hugging students who need human contact to show them they are loved.

It is in this moment that I know, beyond a shadow of a doubt, I have done what is right by my truth. I have stood up to a bully who held the power to destroy not only my career, but my life.

I make two more final promises to myself during that last inter-action with my principal: I will hug every student who needs a hug during the next twenty-one days, and I will tell every teacher who is my friend my truth—THE truth—of my ordeal.

I will tell them during the final three days of the school year, after I have received my rating and immediately after I turn in my resignation. Every teacher in this building deserves to know what a coward and a bully our principal really is on the inside.

I tell Bruce I have nothing left to say to him. I do not accept his apology for "misjudgment." I know I will learn to forgive eventually so that I can move on, but today is too soon.

As Bruce gets up and walks out of my classroom, I stand still and bask in the lightness I feel within. I have stood up for myself, my career, and my life. And Bruce can NEVER take that from me.

May 30
20 Days Left

The Luxury of Oral Surgery

I am getting my wisdom teeth yanked out today. When my dentist informed me a few months ago that it was time, I cried. I'm not sure why. For some reason, I am proud to still have my wisdom teeth at the age of thirty-six. But alas, they are coming out today. I've heard horror stories from some people about getting their wisdom teeth taken out. For others, it has been a breeze. (I'm embracing "the breeze" philosophy.) Michael, my husband, will be going with me for the surgery.

We report to the oral surgeon's office. There seems to be a mix-up once the doctor takes a look in my mouth. He calls my regular dentist and says, "Her wisdom teeth look fine. Why are we doing this procedure?" My dentist informs him that the teeth are pretty much decayed in the centers and must come out.

When, for a split second, I think I might have to go back to school if I don't need the surgery, feelings of sorrow and pain well up inside about my recent ordeal. I decide that if I don't need the oral surgery, I will take today and tomorrow off anyway—I need a break to heal and recharge.

My oral surgeon takes another look, agrees with my dentist that surgery is needed, and we begin. My mouth is prepped and the mask is placed on my face. I am asked to count backwards from ten. "Ten, nine, eight..." the last number I remember.

Two hours later, I am awake and my mouth really does feel fine. I am swollen and bleeding, but there is no pain. My husband and I climb into the taxicab and head home. The rest of the day is spent on the sofa, drifting in and out of sleep. What a luxury!

May 31
19 Days Left

Excruciating Pain

The pain is unbearable. There is no swelling, but the pain—deep inside my jaw and creeping toward the back of my neck—is excruciating. It feels like someone is prying my remaining teeth out, one by one, as slowly as possible.

I try to sit up and that makes it even worse. I lie back, prop myself up on pillows, and open my laptop to check on what's happening in the world. Even that is too much. I try to care about a multitude of things that are important to me right now, but I can't even find the energy to do that.

I resign myself to more lying on the sofa.

June 3
18 Days Left

Adjusting My A-Game

It has been four days since my surgery, and something is terribly wrong. My head is pounding, and my jaws hurt deep into my neck and lower skull. I have spent the last two days icing my face—every vibration and noise sends an excruciating bolt of pain through my face and neck. My doctor's excuse was only for two days, so I will myself to get up, shower, and get ready to teach. Every little movement causes pain like I have never experienced before. I know this day is not going to be easy, but we are in the final eighteen days of the school year and seasoned teachers know that if you show up, you had better deliver your A-game.

I board the F train in Brooklyn. As soon as it pulls out of the station, I realize I've made a terrible mistake: The movement and vibrations of the train make me fear I'll throw up from nausea and pain. By the time I get to school one hour and fifteen minutes later, I know something is terribly wrong. I make a note to call my oral surgeon as soon as his office opens.

In the meantime, I need a survival plan for the day. One of the downfalls of this educational system is that students take standardized state tests in mid-May, but school doesn't let out until the final week of June. It doesn't take a rocket scientist to observe that many students—and, sadly, some teachers—consider the last five weeks of the school year a waste of time. I have never subscribed to this thinking, but many do.

The students file into the room and ask how I am doing. Their inquiries are genuine because they really do care. We have built a mutual relationship based on compassion, love, and respect. All I can do is simply shake my head and lightly "Shh" them until they take their seats and the room is silent. They definitely know their lively teacher isn't feeling so lively today.

"Class, I am in tons of pain. Something is wrong, and I need to call my dentist as soon as his office opens. Today, I don't care what you do, but you must stay seated and quiet because every movement and noise causes me deep pain. Anything above a whisper—like how I am talking now—won't be tolerated. Read a book. Write a story. Do some homework for another class. Whisper with your neighbor. Just please be quiet and good."

I look out across the drop-dead silent room and see both confusion and compassion. My students have never heard me speak such words: They know we spend every single one of our ninety minutes together in productive work mode. I massage my jaws for the only relief I can get from the deep, aching pain. The kids watch me and I am fine with that. I don't perceive anything that I have said or done as a weakness, but just pure honesty. It's how I operate my life inside and outside the classroom.

The first ninety minutes of the day go by without a hitch. The next class files in, I give them the same spiel, and they also do as asked. At lunchtime, I call the doctor. His assistant assures me that what I am experiencing is not normal. I book an appointment for 10:00 tomorrow morning and feel relief already.

June 4
17 Days Left

Exposed Nerves

Dry sockets: This is the diagnosis I have been given. Basically, dry sockets happen when the blood doesn't clot properly in the open cavity, exposing the roots of other teeth to air, food, and beverages. No wonder I've been in so much pain and misery!

Unfortunately, the only thing that can be done for dry sockets is to fill them with clove oil and wait for the body to mend itself. The doctor gives me a bottle of natural clove oil, instructions on how to use it, more gauze to bite on when the pain is intense, and doctor's orders for two additional days of rest and recovery.

I send a text message to my assistant principal and inform him of the news. One of the most wonderful things about the school where I work is when a teacher is sick, he or she is never given grief or made to feel guilty. Philip tells me to rest and get well; I tell him I will send lesson plans via email when I get home.

My colleagues are pretty stellar, too. They pull together the work for my students while I spend the rest of the day sleeping and dreaming about life as a full-time business owner. In seventeen days, I will be calling all the shots.

June 5
16 Days Left

Bids and Paddles

I wake up this morning to find my entire neck, face, and back covered in what appear to be tiny, little whiteheads; it seems I have had an allergic reaction to the antibiotics prescribed for my wisdom teeth. This surgery is more than I bargained for, that's for sure!

This afternoon, I am scheduled to volunteer at The American Heart Association Gala and Fundraiser at the *Intrepid* Sea, Air & Space Museum. My jaw and neck are still pounding, and now I have this rash to conceal for tonight's black tie event.

I am volunteering on behalf of my company, The Writing Whisperer, as part of a select group of business owners who were invited to attend this event. I have only been on the *Intrepid* once, on a day when the museum was bustling with tourists. I'm looking forward to seeing it transformed for a private event.

At 2:00 in the afternoon, I begin the laborious process of assembling myself into an upscale, presentable woman. Normally, this wouldn't be such a big undertaking, but today, with the pain in my jaw and face and my general malaise, I'm feeling sluggish, grumpy, and definitely not my chipper self. However, within an hour, I have showered, fixed my hair, and applied some rosy blush and lip color to my face. Covering the tiny skin abrasions...well, that didn't quite happen.

I arrive at the *Intrepid* at 4:30 in a black cocktail dress, pearl earrings, and strappy black heels. While I am looking the part of a sophisticated lady on the outside, my feet are killing me, my jaw and head are throbbing, and I am getting more and more frustrated with each passing minute as we wait for the event staff to brief us on our duties. The truth is that I should be at home, resting.

I find my fellow business owners, and we catch up on each other's lives. We are then escorted by a young lady in four-inch platform heels through hidden doorways and secret sections of the *Intrepid* where the general public could never navigate on its own. After about five minutes of walking, we arrive in the volunteer section where we and about one hundred other volunteers are given directions on the gala and fundraiser proceedings and what we can expect.

Pizza is delivered for the volunteers to snack on. Honestly, I've never been so happy to see food in my life! Once the aroma hits my nostrils, I realize I am famished; I have not been able to eat much of anything over the past few days. I have no shame in devouring three slices of cheese and mushroom pizza within ten minutes' time.

I have volunteered to help with the silent auction that will take place this evening. My sole responsibility is to make sure my eight guests understand how the silent auction and bidding process will work.

I finish my third slice of pizza, spray some minty breath freshener into my mouth, and go out to meet Table 22, one of the livelier ones in the huge ballroom. I introduce myself and explain how the silent auction will work. Each person is given a paddle marked with his or her name and unique auction number. To bid, they must raise their paddle. If they win, I collect the paddle, and write down the item they bid on and their winning bid.

It seems simple enough to all parties involved, including me.

The lights dim and the music starts. Everyone takes out their glow stick and ignites the festive atmosphere with rainbows of color streaking through the darkness. The energy in the room is contagious and, for the first time in four or five days, I get wrapped up in the moment and forget about my jaw pain.

The auctioneer begins with small-ticket items such as a subscription to a Wine of the Month Club and private tasting parties with notable chefs in their five-star restaurants. I learn rather quickly to pay attention only to my table, or I will miss a bid.

The first bidder from my table wins a Cheese of the Month Club subscription for $750. She is gushing with joy; apparently, cheese is one of her favorite foods. My next bidder is a gentleman dressed in a deep blue pinstriped suit. I imagine him to be the life of the party outside of this formal event as he has a kind smile, is in good spirits, and is joking with his tablemates. He wins a four-night stay at a luxury resort in Buenos Aires with a bid of $4,500 (market value $1,750). I am speechless—$4,500 dollars for a four-night vacation?! I have never before witnessed this amount of wealth.

Finally, the last auction item is announced—six nights in an Italian villa (market value $2,500). Clearly, this is the prize everyone has been waiting for, as the bidding paddles are flying in a frenzy. A quiet man at my table raises his paddle ever so slightly. The auctioneer is calling out the bids, "$4,500 here and $5,000 over there!" The pace slows around $6,500, but the quiet man determinedly raises his paddle again and again. At last, the auctioneer announces, "Sold to the man at Table 22 for $8,000!"

I gather his paddle, record the information, thank everyone for a wonderful evening, and return all the paddles to the collection room.

Honestly, I am floored! Tickets for this American Red Cross fundraiser started at $1,500 a person, and my table alone paid $20,000 for three items this evening. Tonight, I definitely have seen the vast economic difference between the teaching world and a sector of the business world. The dichotomy is astonishing!

All volunteers have been invited to a cocktail reception, but I am in too much pain to attend. I say my goodbyes and treat myself to a taxi ride to my train stop. I flag down a taxi and climb in, relieved to be off my feet. After a four-minute ride, we arrive at the train stop where my cabbie tries to charge me $20.

I tell him, "No." He reduces the price to $17 and I shake my head.

"My final offer: $15," he says.

I tell him, "No, that is unacceptable."

We decide on $10. I hand him the cash—with no extra for a tip. (He tried to swindle me!)

On the train, a feeling of awe washes over me: I just haggled with a cab driver for a fair price on my four-minute ride, yet I just left an event where most didn't think twice about paying $8,000 for a $2,500 vacation. It is in this moment I realize I am not jealous or bitter about what I just experienced, but so grateful to have had the chance to inhabit such a different world for a few hours. If anything, I am returning home awakened to the possibilities of what running my own business could mean for my future.

Fifteen Years in Two Boxes

The only reason I even considered going to work today is because there are no students present, as it is a professional development day. I have a classroom to pack and materials to sort and distribute—and only fifteen days left as a public school teacher.

This day—like others when no students are present—is filled with meeting after meeting after meeting. Some meetings are geared toward wrapping up the school year, some for the eighth-grade promotion celebration, and some for planning the next school year. Honestly, by this time of the year, we teachers are dragging and the last thing we want to think about is planning for next fall.

I know my decision to leave teaching is final, because this year I have hardly packed anything from my classroom to take home. Just five years ago, when I moved from Charlotte to New York City, I brought my files, bulletin board borders, curriculum units, and those books near and dear to me. But today, I leave almost everything. I pack two small boxes with my personal items along with many notes and cards that students, parents, and teachers have written to me over the years.

Since I am not too busy, I offer to help my fellow teachers prepare their classrooms for summer break. I help move furniture. I pack up books and science kits and a year's worth of memories made in their classrooms. And I do share in their excitement for next year's possibilities.

I am not as emotional about my own departure as I thought I might be. If anything, I'm still angry and hurt about the hugging incident. If I think about it for too long, tears well up and spill down my cheeks.

The 145-Step Shuffle

Today is the first day in a week when I haven't felt like my face is going to fall off—I am claiming this as a victory! I report to school, ready to take on the day. I am informed that today I will be teaching my full load of classes and covering an art class. My lunchtime will, once again, be taken from me due to the rain. (When it rains, students can't have recess outdoors, and my administration has yet to figure out another way to ensure that we teachers get our mandatory lunch period.)

On top of having our contract ignored, we end up with antsy students and irritable teachers. What good does this combination serve? The teachers are hungry, don't have time to pee, and are mentally exhausted. The students have to gulp down their lunches in less than twenty minutes and have nowhere to release their energy. It's a bad situation all the way around, and could be fixed so easily if administration would just work with the teachers to devise a new and improved plan.

Today is fire drill number nine of the ten we must conduct every year. If we were in a "flat" school building, it wouldn't be too cumbersome. But because my building is eight floors high and my classroom is on the seventh floor, a fire drill wastes about twenty-two of my forty-four minute teaching period. So, whenever this mandatory procedure is announced, it's certain that my lesson has to be rescheduled.

The fire bell rings and the students groan in unison. I can't say I blame them. Not only is it drizzling outside, but we must embark on the 145-Step Shuffle. We leave the classroom in a single file and take an immediate right. Exiting the seventh floor south doors, we enter the stairwell and head down, gaining speed until we come to a dead halt at the fourth floor. Elementary students, moving slower than molasses, are entering the stairwell too. We wait. My students look at me, roll their eyes, smile secretly. It's been a standing joke all year long that if we did have a fire on our side of the building, we would be doomed when we hit the fourth floor—burned into crispy critters while we wait for the slow students to file out of the building.

We finally make it out of the building, walk across the street, and stand in a line. The cool rain is pattering down, mostly blocked by large trees that shade the sidewalk. A few of the eighth-grade girls are upset because their hair is getting wet, but they are freaking out silently, so all is well.

The all-clear bell rings and we begin the hardest part of the 145-Step Shuffle—the ascent. Yes, you read that right, we must climb up 145 stairs every single time we practice a fire drill. It is dreadful.

As a teacher, my job is to support and inspire. While nothing about this climb makes me feel supportive or inspiring, I choose to take it one step at a time, not making any comments, offering encouragement to those students who must stop on landings to catch their breath.

Overweight students are sweating and panting; students with mild cases of asthma were sure to grab their inhalers before heading down the stairs; and students with lots of energy race each other up to the top. I find them outside the door of the classroom, trying to calm down.

You may think this ends the 145-Step Shuffle. Actually, the worst is yet to come: The room is hot and humid because my air conditioner is not working. Everyone wants to get a drink of water, but we must take turns with the rest of the students on the floor. I distribute paper towels so the students can try to soak up the sweat.

My lesson for today is over; it never really began. I opt to turn off the lights and let everyone read their books by sunlight for the next eighteen minutes. And I notice my jaw is throbbing once again from the steep climb. I can't wait for this day to end so I can go home and crawl into my bed.

June 10
13 Days Left

Two Words That Would Make
All the Difference

We have a half-day with students today! Woo hoo!

On Sunday evening, I received an email from David, a student of mine. I look forward to getting this particular student's emails because his voice is so distinctive—he's sarcastic, yet very respectful. And he is downright hilarious.

The subject line says: I NEED YOUR HELP!!!!!!!!

David writes: "Can I meet you in the morning? I need to finish some work that I left in school. And I know that you will let me into the building. And I can count on you to check your email. Please e-mail me back. Thank you."

My response: "I will be there at a quarter to eight, unless my train is late. Please wait for me on the school's front steps."

David: "Do you mean 7:45 a.m.? Because if that's the case, then here's some advice on how you can be there on time: Leave earlier than normal and I'm sorry if I am sounding a little selfish. But in a way I'm kind of freaking out a little bit. Anyway, thank you for your help."

My response: "Yes, 7:45 a.m. See you then!"

David: "Thank you so much! You are a life saver!"

David is ALWAYS on time. And it just so happens that my train is late. The time is 7:42 a.m.—I know I'm busted. I can only imagine how this is going to go down when I arrive at our meeting place. I briskly walk the five blocks and one avenue to the school, arriving at the front steps at 7:47 a.m. David is standing there, looking at his watch. "Miss, you are two minutes late."

I smile and agree. There are two things I have harped on over the years of my teaching career that apply to this moment: "You will arrive on time for appointments by being early" and "Do what you say you are going to do, when you say you are going to do it."

"David, thank you for being on time and honoring your word. I appreciate you," I state as we ride the elevator up to the classroom.

He smiles and says, "No problem, Miss. I need to get to work now," and runs off to his locker to make right whatever is currently bothering him in his world.

After the students leave for the day, our meetings begin. The state ELA and math preliminary test scores have arrived and we have been called together to discuss them. As I anxiously scan the reports, I realize that out of the fifty-four students I teach, only one did not pass the state ELA test. I am ecstatic and relieved! Many months of hard work by the students and me has paid off, big time. The rigorous lessons my colleagues and I developed to align with the new Common Core Standards have prepared my students well: They are ready to go to high school!

I sit through the rest of the meeting, waiting to hear those two tiny words from my administration—not just for me, but for the entire staff which has worked so hard. The words never come. Instead, their words are about preparing for next year and how to ensure continued growth.

The words "thank you" are rarely said. My heart aches deeply. It would have been so simple and appropriate to acknowledge the staff's hard work. The lack of gratitude in education has been a huge factor in driving me out of the classroom.

Daily Happy Hour to the Rescue

Everyone is starting to get a little squirrelly. My eighth-grade students have mentally checked out and, to be honest, I'm not far behind. In order to survive the last few days of any school year, it's important to start happy hour at home no later than five and to get an ample amount of sleep each night.

We kick off the day by going over all the fun activities coming up for the 2013 eighth-grade class: We send them off in style with a promotion ceremony followed by a cake reception, an eighth-grade awards brunch, a riverboat dance cruise, a formal dance at a Harlem ballroom, and loads of memorable activities. It is so enjoyable for both the staff and the students, albeit absolutely exhausting.

It's time for the students to fill out the music request forms for our cruise. While passing out the slips of paper, we discuss how to complete them. A small buzz of excitement washes over the room, but completely evaporates in a few minutes. I walk around, asking students what the issue is and why their papers are blank.

"Do we have to put "clean" music choices on here?" one student asks. I've been asked this question many, many times. The songs they listen to are filled with vulgarity—words and innuendoes that make my toes curl and my skin turn a deeper shade of pink. I simply ask them to do their best when choosing music. They don't know what that means and neither do I, but it seems to pacify them for the time being.

I walk over to Jay's table. "I've never seen so many people having trouble coming up with music," I state matter-of-factly.

Jay's head snaps up, "Did you just say you've never seen so many people making out in the hallway?"

I look at him and smile. His table busts out laughing. Jay hears what he wants to hear, when he wants to hear it. I've accused him of having severe hearing loss this year. He agrees. Some of the stuff he says just makes me laugh hysterically. This is one example.

I look at my watch. The time is 9:25 a.m. Happy hour starts in exactly seven hours and thirty-five minutes. The countdown to the end of the year has begun!

June 12
11 Days Left

Classroom Lab Rats

It has been an uneventful morning in Room 719. My fifteen-year-veteran-teacher tricks are working: Keep them busy and engaged with interesting projects, play music once in a while, and allow room for lots of jokes and laughter. This is how everyone makes it to the end of a school year happily.

There is a meeting at lunchtime with our union's district representative because the staff is angry and confused about next year's evaluation process. I can't say I blame them. I've never been more grateful to be a "fly on the wall" and just observe today's meeting without having a vested interest in this ongoing battle.

In about nine minutes, the meeting escalates into a screaming match. The physical education teacher is angry that his final evaluation will be based on reading scores, because he has the students in the gym for only ninety minutes a week. I totally see his point.

The art teacher is equally upset but communicates more calmly. His rating will also be attached to reading scores. Further, it has been suggested he should teach art through the social studies content so the students can read more about art history. (Yes, you read that correctly.)

The eighth-grade science teacher is livid. Her evaluation will be based on the eighth-grade science test scores, which measure the students' cumulative knowledge of the science curriculum from fourth to eighth grade.

I completely understand her anger and frustration.

As I sit at my desk, watching the tempers flare, listening to the valid points made by each teacher, witnessing the anger and frustration of my colleagues—a microcosm of the national climate around education—I am literally brought to tears.

The most painful truth of all? Students are sick of being classroom lab rats who are tested every other month in every class so baseline scores can be established, knowledge gains and losses charted, and pilot tests revised once again.

In their effort to ensure efficient use of government funding, politicians frequently increase teacher performance standards to the point where they are unrealistic. And just when we teachers have adjusted our curriculum and teaching methods to succeed in meeting the latest set of standards, another "new and improved" set of standards is established.

These demands are unrealistic and unethical in a system where administrators are cutting back the hiring of teachers, literally cramming thirty-two or more students into each classroom and telling us that is a manageable workload.

In reality, teachers have no voice in the theoretical world of the political and administrative decision-makers: We are not allowed to provide insight into the real-world implications of their policies. Thus, in spite of every effort we make to succeed, we are doomed to fail, because their policies are not based on classroom realities.

The meeting ends only because the bell has rung and the teachers must meet their students for afternoon classes. I watch them leave my room, a little more deflated and a lot more frustrated.

My heart seems to have slowed, weighed down by what I have just witnessed. I take a moment to mutter a prayer of thanks and gratitude for having the courage to change my life course after fifteen years in the educational battle zone.

June 13
10 Days Left

The Promise of New Beginnings

I have scheduled today off to speak at the Women in Weddings Conference in New Jersey. My presentation topic is the powerful and pivotal role words play in business branding.

I leave the house around 7:30 and drive to New Brunswick, New Jersey. The traffic is light, there's a piping hot cup of black coffee sitting in the console, and Seal, one of my favorite artists, is singing in the background. In this moment, I am filled with so much hope and inspiration and gratitude. While driving, I recall the days when I was struggling with a broken marriage in North Carolina; waking up one day with only five dollars to my name and realizing I wasn't in love any more. I remember the raw pain of selling my first home, moving into my own apartment, and starting my life over again, freshly-divorced. I promised myself then that this time, I would live my life the way I wanted to live it, on my own terms, standing in my own truth.

With only ten days remaining in the classroom, I find myself thinking such thoughts frequently. Teaching no longer satisfies something deep within my soul. Working with the students, planning high-quality curriculum, and building close relationships with my coworkers has kept me in teaching this long.

But the constant rowing uphill, having to prove myself every year under new evaluation techniques that are biased and unattainable, and the latest battle against unfounded accusations about an innocent hug, have all taken their toll on me: The magic of the profession has evaporated.

I drive through the tunnel into New Jersey and tears drip onto my black dress. I realize that in ten days I will be free from the heartache of walking into a place where gratitude is almost nonexistent, when it could so easily be fixed by sharing a heartfelt "thank you" once in a while. I realize how truly happy and proud I am that I have decided to take a stand for something I am one hundred percent committed to—my personal happiness—even if it means uprooting my entire life and what I have known for the past fifteen years as a traditional working woman.

I pull into the conference site—a beautiful waterfront hotel— and unload my car. I walk to the entrance with only one thing on my mind: People have paid to hear me speak today! They yearn to know how words can transform their businesses and they are excited to learn from me. I will also enjoy a catered lunch (which I will have time to sit and eat) and conversations with attendees and other presenters, beginning relationships that will last for years.

In a nutshell, I am valued, and I feel it.

As I set up the projector and laptop for my presentation, my phone vibrates in my purse. I pull it out and see that my principal has texted me, "Where are your lesson plans?" I am insulted. Where are my lesson plans?

I text him back, "They are on my desk. They are the only thing on my desk, with all the materials that go with the plans."

I get a text a few minutes later from him that says, "Oh, I didn't think to look there. And please have your resignation ready by tomorrow. I need to free up money in the budget."

I choose not to respond. I have the day off and shouldn't be bothered with the happenings at school. I also decide that my resignation letter will be turned in when I'm damn well ready, not on his deadline, even if he does need to figure out his budget for the following year. Technically, my resignation doesn't need to be handed in until August first. And I would be a fool to turn it in prior to receiving my final evaluative rating, knowing what I have been through this year.

I push the negative thoughts out of my mind and talk to a few members of the audience. We speak about their businesses and what they want to accomplish in the next few years. I am fueled by their passion and emotion, knowing exactly how they feel, because the business I have been building gives me the same benefits and happiness.

My presentation goes well, and several people ask to speak with me at lunch. Everything I wanted for today has happened already—and it's only noon. I am beyond grateful. I am full of love and the promise of new beginnings. Above all, I am thriving in this new role because I am allowed to be the loving, caring, energetic, sometimes crazy, and very excited me. I have arrived.

June 14
9 Days Left

Building School Spirit

For the past three years, I have organized our school's Egg Drop Competition. Turnout the first year was small, mainly because the teachers and students weren't quite sure what it was. But over the last few years, this event has grown into a school-wide celebration with full participation and an assembly to honor all the students' hard work.

The Egg Drop Competition is a creativity and teamwork activity where student teams design and build a protective device for an egg. Their devices—made of cardboard, cotton balls, bubble wrap, etc.—are designed to prevent an egg from breaking when it is dropped from the top of a fourteen-foot ladder onto a cement floor. The competition started four weeks ago when each student team, headed by a teacher, received their supplies and named their team. The names this year are phenomenal—The Eggstreme Team, The Egginators, There Go My Eggo, and The Eggtastics, just to name a few.

The competition happens this morning and I can't wait to see the creative designs. Excitement fills the air as the students begin filing into the auditorium. The competition begins with Philip, the assistant principal, emceeing the event as he does each year. He tells a few jokes to lighten the mood even more. Students love to see him out of his disciplinarian role.

Because we have twenty-one teams competing this year,

a colleague will help me drop eggs from a second ladder. When our ladders are placed on the auditorium stage, we each take half of the egg protectors and climb up our ladders. The entire audience counts down, "Three, two, one!" and we drop all of the egg protectors. Then the most exciting part begins: A designated member of each team opens their device to reveal their egg, hopefully in perfect condition.

The judges stand by, ready to check each egg's condition. Seventy points are awarded if the egg survives and zero points if the egg is cracked or broken. Up to thirty additional points may be awarded for teamwork and team spirit during the preceding four weeks and for the team's presentation to the judges. All teams are competing for the same prize: A bacon, egg, and cheese breakfast with their whole team, the assistant principal, and me.

As the competition ends and the winning team announced, several colleagues approach to say how much they appreciate this event and all the work of organizing it. They also tell me they're sad I won't be back next year and how my energy will be missed. Their kind words bring on a flood of emotion and some tears, and I hug each one. With the principal watching from the sidelines, I approach the winning team of students and hug them all. They are proud of their accomplishment, as they should be, and there is nothing wrong with giving hugs, so I hand them out freely.

The principal doesn't say a word or try to stop me. As the students file out, many more stop for a hug. And I offer them, one by one, generously and without shame or guilt.

Lessons in the Stairwell

I've been helping the class valedictorian prepare his speech for the eighth-grade promotion ceremony. Lee, an extremely shy male student, has grades that are off the charts. But getting him to talk in class—even in small groups or just one-on-one—has been one of my most difficult challenges this year. However, in just a few days, he must stand up in front of a packed auditorium and deliver his speech to his classmates and an audience of about four hundred people.

Lee and I have been working together on this speech during our lunch hour for the past month. Not only is Lee's voice small and weak, he mumbles, each word getting lost somewhere between his tongue and front teeth. Most of my work has been pumping up his confidence while teaching him what to expect, physically and mentally, when he steps onto the stage and looks out at the crowd.

Today, we work in the stairwell—I stand on the seventh floor landing while he stands on the fifth floor landing. To strengthen Lee's vocal projection and improve his enunciation, I have him deliver his speech up the two flights of stairs. When I can't hear him or a word sounds muffled, I tell him to start over. We practice this for a good five minutes. My idea is working—his speech is clearer and his voice stronger with each practice round.

Next, he stands at one end of the seventh-floor hallway while I stand at the other, about sixty feet away, with my back turned towards him. As he delivers his speech, I use hand signals to coach him. If I raise my right hand, it means I can't hear him; if I wave my left hand to the side, it means his words are jumbled. This technique is also very effective, as it forces him to look up often from his script and visually check in with me, a representation of his audience.

Lee has written the most brilliant, motivating, and captivating speech about the difficulties of making friends with his extreme shyness. Most of his speech encourages his classmates to overcome their own personal weaknesses, which he relates to his weak communication skills. I know his message will be well-received, as long as he and I keep working hard so he can find his own voice and story.

June 18
7 Days Left

Self-Defeating Attitudes
Are Not Allowed

Today, I arrive at school a little early to grade my last set of papers. What a freeing feeling! Believe me, over the years, I have secretly wished I was a math teacher instead of an English teacher when it came time to sit down and grade fifty-four three-to-five page essays.

The first class files in and notices something they've never seen before: Scrabble, Boggle, and Taboo board games litter the room. Most of the students are intrigued and excited about doing something out of the ordinary today. I settle the students into their seats and explain how each game is played. Because we live in a world of modern technology and sophisticated electronic gaming systems, my students listen closely, fascinated that I actually have these relics of the past—these were the games I played with my family and friends while growing up.

I believe I have aged myself, in their eyes, by at least one hundred years.

They break into groups, choose the games they want to play, and get started. Because all of these games require making or using words, there is a ton of resistance from the students. I travel around the room hearing mumbled words like "boring," "no animation," and "no sound effects."

I stop the class for a pep talk. "Most of you are struggling right now because of your negative attitudes. You have been dealt a new experience and, instead of believing in yourself and your ability to try something new, you are resisting and shutting down. I won't stand for it. Everyone, get up." They look at me like I've grown two heads, but each student eventually stands up.

"Repeat after me: 'I am good enough. I am open to new ideas. I will try new things in life so that I will grow as a person. I will open my mind to new experiences.'" Most of the students are now smiling and repeating the affirmations. I stop the class: "We won't continue until everyone participates, so if someone next to you is being uncooperative, give him or her some courage. Let's do it again."

A few students nudge reluctant peers and we start over. "Repeat after me: 'I am good enough. I am open to new ideas. I will try new things in life so that I will grow as a person. I will open my mind to new experiences.'"

Everyone says the lines in unison. They sit back down and begin to play again. And do you know what happens? My students start having fun! Once I addressed the issue, rather than ignoring it, and gave them some coaching with positive affirmations, they really got into the idea of trying something new.

As the students play, I notice how difficult it is for many of them to sit still and think, especially when it isn't their turn at play. But I also witness the beautiful transformation of an entire class that was so reluctant to try something new in the beginning but, by the end of class, is so disappointed when the bell rings and it is time to leave.

As the students file out, I hear two of them talking softly under their breath, "I bet this is why Mrs. Hernandez is so good with words. Her parents made her play word games when she was little."

I can't help but smile. I've been able to share another piece of myself with a younger generation.

June 19
6 Days Left

Dressing the Part

Hands down, my favorite day of the entire year has arrived. Today is our eighth-grade trip down the Hudson River on a riverboat cruise. We will leave school around 9:00 this morning, travel by train to Chelsea Pier, and board our boat to dine, dance, and have tons of sweaty, hot fun in the sun.

The students arrive at school out of uniform. This is one of a handful of days when they are allowed to dress in street clothes. They've spent the entire year thinking about what they will wear on the boat today, conferring with friends, exchanging honest wardrobe opinions and suggestions.

It's astounding the amount of behind-the-scenes coaching we teachers give students for a non-uniform day. We answer questions every day about what is and isn't allowed. For example, we must calm the nerves of students who purchased sundresses, but fear they can't wear them because they have spaghetti straps. And explaining the difference between an appropriate pair of shorts and a pair that borders on "trashy" is always an entertaining conversation in my classroom.

I know why we have a strict uniform policy: It makes everyone appear the same, economically speaking, and reduces gang-affiliation issues. While these two reasons are important, I think the school's strict uniform policy is doing more harm than good.

Here's why: I believe in teaching students "in the moment." We learn best by addressing our mistakes and talking through the issues, which leads to a greater understanding in the end.

The problem with a mandatory uniform policy is that it limits the chances we have to teach students about appropriate dress, if they should need some guidance. I firmly believe our students need opportunities to learn how to dress, especially my female students. The media bombards our youth with images of half-dressed women and portrays them as sexy goddesses. If parents aren't teaching their children what is inappropriate dress and teachers don't have a chance to instruct them, our students receive very little guidance on appropriate attire.

Because there is a school uniform policy, there are few opportunities for our students to identify which clothing is appropriate and which is not. And when we have special days, like today, when students are allowed to choose clothing "using their best judgment," their limited knowledge can lead to inappropriate choices. This can set up many students for failure, embarrassment, and ridicule from peers. Those who show up with inappropriate clothing are banned from the trip and given in-school suspension. It's a Catch-22 that could be completely avoided if the uniform policy wasn't so strict to begin with.

Over the years, I've helped to educate my students and prepare them for "out-of-uniform" days" by having them bring in their outfits ahead of time. Some students put on their outfits and snap a picture, that they bring to me for my opinion. I've taught my female students which bra styles work (and which don't) with which styles of blouses and dresses; the importance of nude underwear when wearing white or light-colored pants and skirts; the need to add a thin tank top under shirts that are cut too low; and how to wear skinny pants properly so they don't look like they've been poured into their clothing.

I've taken young ladies shopping for a proper-fitting bra so their breasts aren't spilling out of their shirts. I've taught the boys the importance of wearing a belt, how to match a belt with shoes, and I've tied so many ties in the past fifteen years, it's unreal.

These are valuable lessons students need to know so they can have bright, successful futures. While these lessons are not part of my curriculum, they are part of my philosophy: Superb teachers teach more than what is required; superb teachers think outside the box, knowing that confining rules such as strict dress codes are doing more harm than good; superb teachers work hard behind the scenes to advocate for changes to outdated policies so students are better prepared for the world outside of school.

The sad reality is this: Superb teachers must not make too many waves or they will be viewed as a threat; superb teachers must keep many of their ideas to themselves, especially those that could transform our educational system, or they will be viewed as troublemakers and non-team players. Thus, superb teachers are generally left with three options:

1. Continue being superb and speaking out about the failing system, hoping that we won't make too many waves and lose our jobs;
2. Conform to the mediocrity in education and allow a little part of our hearts die each day;
3. Leave the profession.

This superb teacher refuses to let parts of her die, or live in fear of losing my job for breaking the silence and speaking too boldly. Five days remain.

June 20
5 Days Left

A Loose-Rule Haven

We spend the majority of today's class time preparing the room for my replacement. I divide students into teams to complete a variety of tasks that must be done before I walk out the door on the 26th of June.

The room is a flurry of activity. Several students have been put in charge of taking down bulletin boards, carefully preserving the decorative border so it can be reused by another teacher. The last of the student work is sorted by class and placed into piles so it can be returned.

I've placed a group of eight students in charge of the classroom library—a task I have dreaded at the beginning and end of each and every school year. Because I have written several grants for current literature over the years, I have top-notch literature on my shelves. Students from all grades in our middle school visit my room in hopes of finding the perfect book. I lend them out right and left, never too concerned if they make it back into my classroom because I just want students to read and enjoy the process.

To organize a classroom library and keep it tidy throughout the year is no small task. Over the years, I got super smart and put students in charge of it! New books must be catalogued, labeled with the appropriate reading level, and placed into the proper genre or author bin. Books in the return bin must first be inspected to see if they need a trip to the book hospital (my desk), then placed into the proper bin. And books found throughout the school in lockers, hallways, and various other places must also be gathered and sorted. When you teach a classroom of fifty-four students who are reading one to two books a week, you can see how much help I need in the classroom library!

Two students are removing gum from the undersides of the lab tables serving as desks in my classroom. (I much prefer to have students sitting at tables in collaborative groups rather than in isolated rows of individual desks.) The gum issue is a battle I have never chosen to fight. The school rule is "no gum," but honestly, I have more to worry about than being on gum patrol. I have always told my students that as long as they didn't chew gum like a cow chews its cud, they were fine. And for the most part, there have been very few gum incidents in the fifteen years of my career.

As the "gum patrol" checks each table, they are surprised to find only a few wads. When I ask why this surprises them, they tell me that desks in other classrooms have lots of tacky, wet gobs of gum just waiting to attack unsuspecting students. They say my tables are clean because I allow gum, so there is no need to hide it or stick it under the table out of spite.

I believe there's a lesson here to be learned by all: The more rules enforced in a school environment, the more workarounds students will devise to break them. My classroom became a sort of "loose-rule zone" in many cases. Students were allowed to get up and stretch during class instruction when needed. They could come into class and take off their shoes, if that was how they learned best. If you popped into my room during reading time, you would see students spread out on the floor, curled into the corners of the room, or reading under the tables. The more freedom I gave them, the better they performed; the more laughter we shared, the fewer behavioral problems we had.

I quickly scan the room—students are laughing, some are playing games, some are finishing the tasks they volunteered to do. For the first time, I feel something stir within me and a brief thought crosses my mind: Are you sure you want to leave this profession?

I take a moment to acknowledge that thought, and then the sound of the bell snaps me back to the here and now. It's lunchtime and it's raining, which means that I'll have to battle for a spot at the only microwave in the building to heat my lunch, most likely I will not get a chance to use the restroom, and I will be spending my lunch hour with students who are as upset and frustrated as I am for having altered lunch plans once again.

Do I want to leave this profession? Perhaps not. Is it time for me to leave this profession? I answer with a definite "Yes."

Hugs for All

This morning is our eighth-grade awards brunch. Students and their families will arrive at the community center we rent for this occasion around 9:00. It will be another full day of hugging, I affirm, as I approach the school building.

Much must be accomplished before the students get here. My colleagues and I arrive earlier than usual, fill carts with food, drink, awards and certificates, table decorations and fresh flowers, and a variety of other items that must be rolled two blocks down the street to the community center. Every year, the awards brunch seems better and bigger than the previous year's celebration.

We get to work arranging tables, moving chairs, setting up the sound system, and decorating the space. In a matter of forty minutes or so, the once-empty room has a festive look and is ready to welcome students and their families. The food has arrived and smells wonderful; this year we have bagels, deli trays, fruit and vegetable platters, and a variety of sweet treats.

We help everyone to be seated and quiet, and then the awards ceremony begins. Teachers have worked hard behind the scenes to spread "the award wealth" throughout the student body as much as possible. Awards are given to students for achievements in academics, clubs, sports, and for community service and personal citizenship qualities.

As the award ceremony ends, I breathe a sigh of relief; last year, one parent was so upset her child didn't get an award she made a scene and walked out. This year, everyone is smiling and ready to eat.

I spot Lee's family across the room and walk over to chat with him and his parents. In just three days, Lee will deliver his valedictory speech, on which he has worked extremely hard. In my eyes, he is already a success because he has come so far in the past few weeks. I share this sentiment with his mother and father and they assure me he will be practicing over the weekend. I know he is going to completely blow away his classmates and teachers, all who have expressed concern about his ability to speak in public because he is so quiet in the classroom. I give him a final hug of encouragement and continue making my rounds to hug more students and share more positive words with parents.

Several parents approach me during the morning to express their gratitude and love for me and for the time I have spent working with and encouraging their children this year. They know I am leaving the profession in a few days and take the time to speak with me and wish me well. Many lament I won't be around for a few more years to teach their younger children. I feel honored by their votes of confidence. I hug every single parent and student I speak with, and the hugs are all returned with open arms, lots of affection, and some tears.

As the students and families file out, we tear down everything we worked so hard to set up. We load the carts again, stack the furniture where we found it, and make sure the kitchen is clean and the garbage stowed away. We begin our walk back to the building where we will spend the rest of the day reviewing all the details for Monday morning's promotion ceremony and finalizing plans for Monday evening's formal dance in Harlem.

My ultimate goal this weekend is to rest. The last three days of the year are a flurry of exciting, rewarding, and enjoyable activities, but they're downright exhausting. During these last three days, I will also break the silence about my misconduct allegation. I will meet with those teachers whom I trust and admire, tell them about the misconduct charge, and inform them that the allegations were unfounded. They need to know what type of person the principal really is and just exactly for whom they are working.

June 24
3 Days Left

My Specialty as a Teacher

The auditorium is overflowing with people and excitement—there is standing room only. I spot Lee as he enters the room and he looks great. Dressed in a pinstriped suit, black shoes, and a crisp white shirt and tie, he looks absolutely, one hundred percent, ready to deliver his speech from the stage.

"Lee, you are looking sharp. How are you feeling?" I ask.

"Fine," he replies; he has always been a student of few words.

"Now remember, you are a success already. People will be tuned in to what you have to say. You are one of the stars of the show today," I encourage. Lee smiles and nods. "What do you need from me right now, Lee?" My main goal is to make him as at ease as possible.

He doesn't need anything, but does want to see where I will be sitting. So I take him over to stage right and show him the second-row seat I reserved for myself to give him an unobstructed view of me from the podium. I will use two hand signals to communicate during his speech, if needed: My hand next to my ear will indicate Lee needs to speak louder; my hand held with the palm facing Lee, placed in front of my chest, will signal he needs to slow down his delivery.

Lee and I have discussed many times the distractions he should expect: babies crying, cell phones ringing, and lots of noise while he is speaking. We have practiced the proverbial pause to add emphasis at certain points in the speech, as well as how to move closer to the microphone if I indicate he needs to speak louder. We check the binder on the podium once again to reassure him that his typed speech is in it. And then we are instructed to take our seats so the promotion ceremony can begin. The ceremony should last around an hour and Lee will take the stage about thirty-five minutes into the event.

For the first time in my life, I feel what I imagine most mothers and fathers must feel when their child takes the stage for a speech, talent show, or any other performance that has required tons of practice. I am nervous for Lee. My heart is beating a little bit faster and my palms are a little sweaty.

Lee is introduced by the previous speaker. He stands up confidently, takes the stairs at stage left, walks to the podium, adjusts the microphone. He looks out over the crowd and smiles. And then he begins. My breath catches in my throat. I remind myself to inhale.

His words flow freely. He is loud, clear, and the pace is perfect. He glances my way to check in with me; I smile and nod. His words about working hard in life to overcome obstacles have captivated his classmates. Six rows of attentive students are hanging onto every single word Lee speaks. Nearby staff members reach over to pat me on the back. They give me the thumbs-up sign. One whispers in my ear, "Wow. How in the hell did you manage to get him to speak like that?" I acknowledge the compliments with a nod and continue to listen.

Lee flips to page three of his speech, pauses, and looks somewhat confused. (Only I notice, because I am so familiar with his mannerisms.) He takes a deep breath, flips to page four, and begins again. I learn later that some of his pages were out of order, but he handles the snafu with professionalism and dignity far beyond his age. As his speech draws to a close, I notice how relaxed he seems behind that podium; he has adopted the stance and demeanor of a public figure who has been addressing crowds and influencing others for years. And just four weeks ago, I was having trouble getting him to speak in class! Today, he has written, delivered, and completely wowed an audience of four hundred people.

He delivers his final line and looks out at his peers, who erupt in a round of applause. He looks over at me and I give him two thumbs-up. As Lee exits the stage and takes his seat, I feel the tears roll down my cheeks.

Never have I been so proud of a student and his hard work to overcome his fear of public speaking, a fear that paralyzes most adults. Lee, at the age of fourteen, has just proven to himself that he can write a speech that influences and captivates a crowd, and he has stood up and delivered it, despite his fear of public speaking.

The ceremony comes to a close and I make a beeline for Lee. His face explodes into a smile and he gives me a hug and thanks me for all of my work to help him prepare for this day.

"Lee, you blew people away. How do you feel right now?" I ask, giving him a firm handshake.

"Fine," his standard reply.

"Want to do it again tomorrow?" I prod.

"No." Lee states firmly, a grin spreading across his face. We find his parents and they, too, are beaming with pride. I give them a final hug, thanking them for all their hard work preparing and practicing the speech at home.

After the ceremony, I deliberately remain behind so I can be one of the last to file out of the auditorium. I look back one final time at the stage and podium and record the image of Lee standing there, tall and confident, speaking to the audience.

My mantra as a teacher has always been, "I teach students, not subjects." My specialty and gift over these years has been elevating students emotionally—supercharging them with affirmations and confidence and the ability to believe in themselves—so they can overcome their personal obstacles. I have never emphasized the subject matter or the standardized test: That doesn't work. What does work is caring, loving, and helping students to understand who they are as individuals, why they are unique and beautiful, and how to set goals and achieve them in life.

As I close the auditorium door, I stand a little taller and a little prouder, too. I haven't caved in to the failing educational system, I haven't lost sight of my values and gifts, and I haven't thrown in the towel and quit. Yes, I am resigning in two days, but my work in education is so far from done. These are the final thoughts I pack up and carry with me as I walk toward the elevator and push the number seven.

June 25
2 Days Left

My West

The heat today is oppressive. The thermometer reads close to ninety-two degrees and it's only 9:00 in the morning.

Last night was the eighth-grade formal dance, and a wonderful time was had by all. Students dressed in their best. Many girls arrived at the ballroom in platform heels and prom-style dresses. The boys were a little more eclectic in tastes; some showed up in khaki shorts and button-down shirts, others in jeans and t-shirts. It was a sight to see, mainly because I was able to witness each student expressing his or her personality through clothing.

Most of us teachers didn't get home until after 11:00 last night. And, as today is optional for students, only thirty or so show up. Our plan is to walk over to Central Park and let the students play in the meadow or on the playground or run through the sprinkler system.

We get to the park and set up our home base. The students are set free, but must stay within eyesight. Most choose to plop down under the shade tree with the six teachers who plan on doing little else for the next two-and-a-half hours. We are exhausted from all the activities of the past weeks, the end of another school year, and the stifling heat.

I spread out my beach towel and lay on my back. Two female students join me and we have a grand time trying to make images out of the puffy, white clouds floating against the blue backdrop.

"Aren't you going to miss us?" one of the girls asks.

"Well, of course, I'm going to miss you. But you are going to high school, so I wouldn't see you much anyway," I confirm.

"Yes, but what about the sixth and seventh graders? We all wait to see if you are listed on our schedule. You are famous!" another student states. I chuckle.

"Well, there are many great teachers at this school and the students will be fine. And anyway, I have a book to write and a business to grow." I look at each of them. They both nod in agreement.

"Do you think we will make it into your book?" they ask, almost in unison.

"I am pretty sure you will," I answer. We all sit up, hug, and the girls run off to find some water.

I lie back down and gaze up at the sky. I see a cloud floating by that I instantly recognize as an arrow, pointing west. My breath catches in my chest.

The westerly direction represents so much in my life. People throughout history have always "headed west" to create a new life, to claim a piece of land as their own. The sunset is one of nature's gifts from which I draw power and clarity in decision-making. When I need to think through decisions in life, I most often do so facing west, watching the sun go down, the sky ablaze with life and color. I close my eyes and reopen them to find the arrow-shaped cloud in the sky. In this moment, I know two things are certain: First, that arrow in the sky is not a coincidence, and second, my west is waiting on me.

June 26
My Last Day

Freedom

I am startled out of sleep by my alarm clock. This is the last day I will set an alarm for 5:15 in the morning. I roll over in bed, give my husband a hug and kiss, and tell him "thank you" for believing in me and supporting me while I build a new future. He is not a morning person. He snuggles in close to let me know he has heard me, gives me a kiss, and drifts off to sleep. He has just given me the fuel I need to get ready for my final day as a public school teacher.

There is almost one hundred percent attendance at school today, even though the day is optional for our eighth-grade class. School will be dismissed at 10:30 this morning. Our last couple of hours together will be spent sharing stories, writing in yearbooks, shedding a few tears. The most important item on my agenda is to complete our year with many kind words and numerous hugs.

As my eighth-grade students leave the building for the last time with a heightened anticipation of their summer break, we say our farewells on the sidewalk behind the school building. I walk with them down to the corner, and then to the next corner, to ensure they are safe from the neighborhood bullies who know our school is releasing early and are waiting for them. I continue walking with them to the train and bus stops, especially the students who are particularly nervous that trouble may find them.

After they are all as safe as I can ensure, I head back to the school building. I have decided to break my silence today, after I have signed off on my final evaluative rating. I walk into the office to view the evaluation. It's marked with a single "S" for Satisfactory, as it has been every year of my career. I've received a Satisfactory rating—the one teachers expect to see—rather than a "U" which would mean a year of unsatisfactory performance.

I sign the paper and wonder how it can be that my entire year—with all the hard work I put in with my students, including weekends and evenings—can boil down to an "S" rating. It's so black and white. You are either satisfactory or you are not. There is no room to award an "above and beyond" teacher anything more than a "S." I find this very sad; yet another symbol of the mediocrity under which the public education system operates.

I make a copy of the rating for my files and hand in my signed resignation letter to the principal (who is on the phone and merely nods and smiles). I walk to my classroom and pack the evaluation in my book bag so it's safe.

Then I begin making my rounds to several teachers to explain exactly what I have gone through since May 8, when I received the letter of misconduct. I cry with each teacher I tell. And they join me in the tears, in the pain, in the anger at a man with such poor judgment who is in a position to run a school. None of us understand why he would have severed and disrespected our relationship by filing that report without first talking with me.

Each teacher with whom I break the silence gives me a warm embrace and thanks me for telling my story. A few share that they, too, know the pain, as they were also reported by our principal on bogus misconduct charges. And while shared experience may be comforting to some, it just makes me very sad. There is nothing comforting about the injustice dealt to many teachers because of the warped mind of one supervisor.

The staff gathers for a catered lunch in the art room, and those of us who are leaving are presented with gifts and flowers. My colleagues fully expect me to give a speech when my name is called, like the others do, but I do not. My emotions today span from pride for what I have accomplished in the past fifteen years, to the relief of being free of a failing system and hope for a fulfilling future. I accept my flowers and gifts with gratitude and return to my seat.

My dear friend Philip, the assistant principal, the person who has fought for every single request I have made in the past four years, leans over and whispers, "I was sure you would give a speech." Tears well up in my eyes and trickle down my cheeks. I slowly shake my head and reply, ever so softly, so only he can hear, "I have a book to write."

He nods, smiles, and I know that, as always, I have his support. I walk to my classroom, pack my gifts, and look around Room 719 one last time. I have not given up. I have not quit. I have followed my truth, which speaks so loudly from within and is rooted core-deep in my spirit: I deserve a life I love, where I wake up every single day, excited about the possibilities and experiences that await me, and one in which I feel valued, appreciated, and noticed.

I head west down the hallway to the bank of elevators. I exit the building and walk west toward the train station. I take a deep, cleansing breath and I look into the sky, toward the west, at the sun. I murmur a prayer of gratitude and descend underground.

My west has begun.

Afterword

To wrap up this part of my journey for you, I first need to take you back, way back before I ever set foot into a classroom.

When I was a child, I dreamed about becoming a teacher. I would line up my stuffed animals and dolls alongside my little sister and teach for hours. I would create worksheets, demonstrating how to read and do simple math problems while writing on the chalkboard in my room. Teaching was what I always wanted to do. It was my dream. It was my truth.

I made that dream come true, and lived in it for fifteen years. When that dream died, it did not go gently; facing the death of a dream is never easy. When I started thinking about leaving my teaching career, the tug of war between my head and heart was the most difficult part of the whole decision-making process.

My head rationalized all the reasons to stay: You've been teaching for fifteen years. It's what you know. It's a steady paycheck with benefits. What are you thinking, Shannon?

My heart countered: You aren't happy. Do you really want to live this way for the next fifteen years? This profession is not what it used to be—it's time to dream bigger, Shannon.

But once I made the decision to leave teaching—that was it. I knew I would find a way to make it happen and never look back.

I spent weeks thinking about ways to reinvent myself. I have often said to others that teaching is a very secluded profession. As a teacher, I reported to school each day, welcomed my students, and then shut the door to teach. There was very little time for socializing during the school day. After school, many teachers were running to their clubs and sports, or leaving to pick up their own children. In addition to the loneliness and isolation I felt, there weren't many opportunities for advancement. If you didn't want to be a teacher, your next step was to be an administrator. And if you didn't want to be an administrator, you remained a teacher.

Fifteen years submerged in the teaching profession made it very difficult to rethink my life. I had forgotten how to dream; I only knew what it was to be a teacher and how to teach. After much thought and reflection, I made a list of those things I wanted most when I reemerged as a business owner:

- A flexible daily schedule that allows time for all the things I love—exercising, writing, time with friends, and naps
- Breakfast and yoga with my husband and cat each morning
- A four-day workweek
- A seven-hour workday
- The ability to travel when I want and for as long as I want
- A proper lunch hour, complete with healthy, freshly-cooked food
- To work in and cultivate an environment ruled by love and compassion, before anything else
- Bathroom breaks when the urge hits!
- To write professionally
- To make a difference in the lives of others
- And to change the world, a little each day, through positive and uplifting words

In the end, I didn't have to give up my dreams at all. Rather, I had to learn to dream bigger than I ever thought was possible, so I could create the bigger life and career that was calling to me. When I contemplated this deeply, I realized there were numerous ways I could teach and inspire others outside of a school classroom.

As it's turned out, almost all of the services I have designed for my business, The Writing Whisperer, involve teaching others about the various aspects of personal and business writing. Because I shifted the direction of my dream, I now have the best of both worlds: the ability to continue teaching and inspiring others and the personal and professional happiness I was so desperately seeking.

In the weeks following my final day as a public school teacher, I didn't have it within me to share any of that. I was often asked how I felt. Did I think I made the right decision? What did it feel like to walk out of the school building for the final time? And what was my plan if I wanted to return?

To be honest, I was still housing so much pain and grappling with the heartbreak over the hugging incident, all I could tell people was that I felt relieved. Wisely, Michael and I went on a vacation shortly after the school year ended. We took a very long road trip, which was instrumental in facilitating the healing needed for my broken spirit. We drove down the East Coast to Edisto Island, South Carolina where, by the gorgeous ocean, we shut out most of the world for eight days and invested in our relationship. I am convinced it was one of the best things I could have done, as it made a clean break between the ending of the old dream and the absolute commitment to the new one, with no Plan B.

Now, I am living an entirely new life. My days start with excitement—breakfast and yoga with my husband, and playtime with my cat—and end with a smile and pure happiness. I am traveling to places I have never been before, both stateside and across the world, and sharing new experiences with my husband, strangers, and friends. I am creating programs for my business that help others heal through journaling and help them build their own businesses. I have the time and energy to explore the things I want to learn more about, like art journaling and the unique ecosystem of city life. I am training for a marathon, I am volunteering for causes I am most passionate about, and I am meeting new people every day.

These interactions fuel my soul by helping me to dream even bigger and learn more about the world I live in. One of the most fulfilling aspects of my new life is this: Each day I receive at least one "thank you" from someone who appreciates how I have helped or impacted them. I cherish these two words dearly and will never take them for granted.

Are you on a quest for something "better?" If you are, my sincere hope is that you continue to explore the new life you so deeply yearn for. Whether you are working to improve yourself or your career, solve a problem or influence many people, it all begins with a dream. Once that dream is born in your heart, it will be time to take action. Try making a list of those special things you want to have in your reinvented life. Expect some internal struggles as you shift away from old beliefs and embrace the new. Be sure to root all action on your journey in love, understanding, and compassion, and always be open to new ideas.

A new life filled with passion and pure happiness is available to you! Break the silence and use your voice for positive change. And once all of the pieces are in their proper places, head west—. I will be waiting for you.

On the following pages, I have included several resources which will assist you along your journey to something "better." If you are a concerned parent or hold a position related to public education, and are yearning for something better for our nation's failing school system, there are resources for you. Likewise, if you are searching for a way to reinvent yourself to find personal and professional happiness, I have included those resources I found most helpful along my own journey.

I invite you to connect with me via my website at www.myfinal40days.com or write me at the address below. I would love to read your inspiring words as you put your dream into action and head west.

Shannon Hernandez
P.O. Box 150-198
Brooklyn, NY 11215

Resources for the Educational Community

All change begins with dialogue; most often, an internal realization that something just doesn't align with our core values and truths anymore. Once we take the time to explore these inner thoughts and emotions, we will then break our silence and share them with a trusted friend, family member, or colleague.

My close friends—many of whom are teachers and college professors—have often broken the silence with me, asking me to offer solutions to the educational problems I raise in this book. I have conferred with public school teachers across the country, professors at the university where I teach, and parents who want a better learning environment for their children. Thus, over the past few years, I have given much thought to the failures of America's education system.

While I don't know all the answers, I do know that education reform will never be successful if we continue to shut out the voices of teachers across this nation. I also know that real reform begins at the local level. It is going to require that school board members, administrators, teachers, parents, and students gather to have meaningful conversations about the need for reform in school tone, curriculum, and leadership.

If you are willing to initiate discussions in your community, a good starting point is the five main issues I spoke about in this book:

1. **We have stopped educating the whole child.** There is no consideration given to, or time allocated for, teaching essential life skills which will help our children to be successful in the world after school. In addition, creative outlets for students such as art, music, science, and physical education classes continue to be eliminated so more time can be allotted for tested subjects.

2. **Teachers are overworked and challenged by poor working conditions, resulting in productivity loss.** Teachers are expected to churn out well-educated students from overcrowded, underfunded classrooms with very little administrative support. Most workdays begin before sunrise and end well after sunset. After the workday "ends," there are papers to grade, parents to call, students to email about assignments, and lesson plans to prepare. Teachers rarely leave school empty-handed, because there are never enough hours in the school day to do all that is required. And the cold, hard truth is that those teachers who manage to eat lunch and use the restroom during the school day are the lucky few.

3. **Standardized testing is the primary focus of education, not educating children.** The expected outcomes are simply not realistic for teachers, students, or schools for a variety of reasons. When a single test score is the criterion for success, and it is based on the premise that the students' learning behavior can be managed and measured without having control of all the variables (such as whether a student lives in a safe and supportive environment and comes to school regularly), the system has failed.

4. **Policymakers are severely disconnected from the realities of the classroom** and the limitations under which most teachers operate, yet they continue making decisions that impact the daily life of every student and teacher in this country. If policymakers consulted with the experts in classroom education—teachers—their initiatives would be more effective and successful.

5. **We, as a society, have lost respect for our teachers and their integral role in our society's success.** We live in a world that tends to idolize professional sports players and celebrities instead of the education professionals who have a very influential role in shaping the future of this nation.

In addition to your involvement in local discussions, I encourage you to explore the list of resources below. Contact the organizations you're interested in and see how you can become more involved. Visit the websites and read the books and journal articles for a deeper understanding of our current educational challenges.

For Teachers

Badass Teacher Association (BAT)
www.badassteacher.org
The BAT is for every teacher who refuses to be blamed for the failure of our society to erase poverty and inequality, and refuses to accept assessments, tests, and evaluations imposed by those who have contempt for real teaching and learning.

Diane Ravitch
www.dianeravitch.com
Diane Ravitch is a Research Professor of Education at NYU, as well as an educator, historian, and author. She served as Assistant Secretary of Education in the early 1990s and has authored ten books. She continues to be a leading voice in education reform and a proponent of better education for all.

The National Center for Fair & Open Testing (FairTest)
www.fairtest.org
FairTest advances quality education and equal opportunity by promoting fair, open, valid, and educationally-beneficial evaluations of students, teachers, and schools. FairTest also works to correct the flaws in testing practices and end the misuse of testing.

The Network for Public Education (NPE)
www.networkforpubliceducation.org
The NPE is an advocacy group whose mission is to protect, preserve, promote, and strengthen public schools and the education of current and future generations of students.

Truth in American Education (TAE)
www.truthinamericaneducation.com
TAE is a grassroots network whose mission is to bring awareness to the government's behind-the-scenes efforts to drastically alter American education. It advocates that all major educational changes be subject to an open and public discussion prior to approval and implementation.

For School Administrators

Facilitative Leadership Training Institute
www.facilitativeleader.com
The Facilitative Leadership Training Institute teaches leaders to respectfully elicit the insights, creativity, and wisdom from others, creating an environment where each member of the group profoundly respects the wisdom and contributions of others.

Demystifying Professional Learning Communities: School Leadership at Its Best by Kristine Hipp and Jane Bumpers Huffman
The authors of this book clearly define an approach to school improvement that uses professional learning community (PLC) practices to achieve school improvement and success for every student. Case studies found within the book clarify the concept of a PLC, and support educational leaders in responding to critical issues in schools, such as addressing the important mandates of accountability and school improvement.

Leadership is an Art by Max De Pree
Max De Pree looks at leadership as a type of stewardship and stresses the importance of building quality relationships, initiating ideas, and creating a value system within an organization. He shows that the first responsibility of a leader is to define reality and the last is to say "thank you."

Love Works: Seven Timeless Principles for Effective Leaders by Joel Manby
Joel Manby, a highly successful corporate executive, introduces readers to the power of love in the workplace. He challenges leaders to allow integrity and faith to guide leadership decisions, outlining seven time-proven principles that work.

Smart Leaders, Smarter Teams: How You and Your Team Get Unstuck to Get Results by Roger M. Schwarz
Organizational psychologist and leadership consultant Roger Schwarz reveals how leaders can drastically improve results by changing their individual and team mindsets.

For Parents

The National Center for Fair & Open Testing (FairTest)
www.fairtest.org
FairTest advances quality education and equal opportunity by promoting fair, open, valid and educationally beneficial evaluations of students, teachers and schools. FairTest also works to end the misuses and flaws of testing practices that impede those goals.

Rethinking Schools
www.rethinkingschools.org
Rethinking Schools is firmly committed to equity and to the vision that public education is central to the creation of a humane, caring, multiracial democracy.

The Bartleby Project
www.bartlebyproject.com
Alongside your child, join the Bartleby Project and peacefully refuse to participate in standardized test preparation or standardized testing.

The Network for Public Education (NPE)
www.networkforpubliceducation.org
The NPE is an advocacy group whose mission is to protect, preserve, promote, and strengthen public schools and the education of current and future generations of students.

Truth in American Education (TAE)
www.truthinamericaneducation.com
TAE is a grassroots network whose mission it is to bring awareness to the government's behind-the-scenes efforts to drastically alter American education. It advocates that major educational changes be subject to an open and public discussion prior to approval and implementation.

For Teacher Preparation Programs

Twenty Questions about Cogenerative Dialogues in Transforming Urban Education: Urban Teachers and Students Working Collaboratively by Kenneth Tobin, et al. 2014.
This chapter explores twenty central questions that relate to the development and use of cogenerative dialogue as a means of improving the quality of teaching and learning, getting to know the culture of others in a classroom, and establishing a place for the practice of critical pedagogy.

Relationships Between Emotional Climate and the Fluency of Classroom Interactions by Kenneth Tobin, et al. 2013.
This study examined emotional climate in relation to the teaching and learning of grade seven science. The methods we pioneered in the present study might be helpful for other teachers who wish to participate in research on their classes to ascertain what works and should be strengthened, and identify practices and rituals that are deleterious and in need of change.

*Learning the "Boundaries:" Racial Listening, Creationism, and Learning from the "Other".*by K. Alexakos, et al. 2013.
In our forum's contribution to Federica Raia's manuscript (2012) on learning at the boundaries, we propose that using radical listening in the science education classroom, especially when contentious issues such as evolution are discussed, helps stakeholders learn from each other's values and viewpoints and contributes to bridging divides.

Letters to a Young Teacher by Jonathan Kozol
Jonathan Kozol, through this personal, insightful, and revealing book, takes readers on a journey through his encouraging letters to Francesca, a young teacher who is struggling with outrage at the inadequacies of America's educational system.

There Are No Shortcuts by Rafe Esquith
Rafe Esquith's candor and uncompromising vision in his fifth-grade classroom in a Los Angeles inner-city school, known as the Jungle, has led him to create lifelong learners who read passionately, tackle algebra, and stage Shakespeare plays like professionals.

For Education Policy Makers

Confessions of a Bad Teacher: The Shocking Truth from the Front Lines of American Public Education by John Owens
John Owens left a lucrative job to teach English at a public school in New York City's South Bronx, thinking he could do some good. Instead, as his students began to thrive under his tutelage, Owens found himself increasingly mired in a broken educational system driven by broken statistics, finances, and administrations undermining their own support system—the teachers.

The Death and Life of the Great American School System: How Testing and Choice Are Undermining Education by Diane Ravitch
Drawing on over forty years of research and experience, Diane Ravitch critiques today's most popular ideas for restructuring schools, including standardized testing, punitive accountability, privatization, and the influx in charter schools. Conclusively, she shows why the business model is not an appropriate way to improve schools.

The Flat World and Education: How America's Commitment to Equity Will Determine Our Future by Linda Darling Hammond
Linda Darling Hammond offers an eye-opening wake-up call concerning America's future. She vividly illustrates what the United States needs to do to build a system of high-achieving and equitable schools that ensures every child the right to learn.

Why Great Teachers Quit: And How We Might Stop the Exodus
by Katherine (Katy) Farber
More talented teachers are leaving the profession than ever before. Katherine Farber, through a series of in-depth interviews, presents an in-the-trenches view of the classroom exodus and offers solutions for how schools can turn the tables and create an environment that fosters teacher retention.

Resources for Those Seeking Reinvention

I've learned, firsthand, that it takes self-reflection, determination, compassion, and massive doses of courage and support to reinvent yourself, once you have decided to take action and make your new dream a reality. For you, breaking the silence might mean starting at the core-level of your soul, and having a stern talk with yourself about why you are not currently happy and lack fulfilment on your current path. Perhaps you may have to go even deeper, as I did, and learn to dream again. Please know that wherever you are right now, there are people who can be of great help to you.

On the following pages is a list of resources that will be instrumental in the process of reinventing yourself. There are countless others, but I encourage you to start here.

Books for Reinventing Work

Coach Yourself to a New Career: 7 Steps to Reinventing Your Professional Life by Talane Miedaner

Talane Miedaner provides the tools necessary to take matters into your own hands and assess your strengths and needs. Once this crucial step is complete, Miedaner then guides readers through finding the right work fit, weighing options and possible sacrifices, and preparing their family for transitions.

Do What You Love, The Money Will Follow: Discovering Your Right Livelihood by Marsha Sinetar

In this step-by-step guide to finding the "work" that expresses and fulfills your needs, talents, and passions, Marsha Sinetar shows how to overcome fears and take the tiny risks that make the big risks possible, through the use of dozens of real-life examples. The end result is that you will become a person whose work means self-expression, growth, and love!

Life Reimagined: Discovering Your New Life Possibilities by Richard J. Leider and Alan M. Webber

Are you at a point in your life where you're asking, "What's next?" Leider and Webber have written this book as a map to guide you in this new life phase. Not only will you be inspired by the ordinary people who have reimagined their lives in extraordinary ways, but you will also uncover your own special gifts, connect with people who can support you, and explore new directions.

Books for Reinventing Life

Daring Greatly: How the Courage to be Vulnerable Transforms the Way We Live, Love, Parent, and Lead by Brené Brown
Researcher and thought leader Dr. Brené Brown offers a powerful new vision that encourages us to dare greatly. Daring greatly means we must embrace vulnerability and imperfection, live wholeheartedly, and courageously engage in our lives.

Jump...and Your Life Will Appear: An Inch-by-Inch Guide to Making a Major Change by Nancy Levin
Nancy Levin's book gives readers the courage and faith needed to jump across the threshold from where they currently are to where they want to be. *Jump...and Your Life Will Appear* is a step-by-step guide to clearing the path ahead so you can let go and make the change you need the most. Using a series of effective exercises, Levin walks you through your fear, ushers you up to the moment of jumping, and helps you navigate what awaits on the other side.

Love Yourself Like Your Life Depends On It by Kamal Ravikant
Kamal Ravikant, guides readers through his personal transformation with this collection of thoughts on what he has learned, where he has succeeded and failed, and what has worked and hasn't. Ravikant shows readers how to love ourselves with the same intensity we would use to pull ourselves up if we were hanging off a cliff with our fingers—as if our lives depended upon it.

Take Time for Your Life: A Personal Coach's 7-Step Program for Creating the Life You Want by Cheryl Richardson
Cheryl Richardson's strategies show you how to step back, regain control, and make conscious decisions about the future you'd like to create, whether you're a single parent trying to raise a family, someone starting a business, a corporate executive working sixty hours a week, or going back to school. Richardson teaches how to overcome the obstacles that block you from living the life you want and helps you discover a world in which your priority list reflects your true desires.

The Right Questions: Ten Essential Questions to Guide You to an Extraordinary Life by Debbie Ford

Debbie Ford's book reminds us that the realities of the life we live today are a result of the repeated, unconscious choices we made yesterday, three months ago, and three years ago. Ford cuts right through our denial with ten questions that immediately reveal the true motivations behind our thoughts and actions. By rigorously and honestly working through these ten vital questions, we regain control and have the power necessary to create the life we always wanted.

Thrive: The Third Metric to Redefining Success and Creating a Life of Well-Being, Wisdom, and Wonder by Arianna Huffington

In this deeply personal book, Arianna Huffington talks candidly about her own challenges with managing time and prioritizing the demands of a career and raising two daughters. In fact, this hectic lifestyle led to her personal wake-up call, which appeared in the form of a broken cheekbone and a nasty gash over her eye, brought on by exhaustion and lack of sleep. Drawing on the latest research and scientific findings, Huffington shows us the way to a revolution in our culture, our thinking, our workplace, and our lives, through the profound and transformative effects of meditation, mindfulness, unplugging, and giving.

Organizations, Programs, and Coaches

Dream University—www.dreamuniversity.com
DreamU exists to provide the tools, resources, and classes needed to make any personal or professional dream come true.

Rockport Institute—www.rockportinstitute.com
Rockport Institute is a worldwide leader in helping people choose and design careers they love.

Anastacia Brice—www.anastaciabrice.com
Anastacia Brice is a foundations coach. She helps her clients uncover or reclaim the truths of who they are, the work they want to do, and the lives they want to live, and then rides shotgun on their journeys as they create what's next for them. (Tell her I sent you!!)

Melinda Emerson—www.succeedasyourownboss.com
Melinda Emerson, known as SmallBizLady, is America's #1 small business expert, and she has one single mission threaded throughout her work: to end small business failure.

Tai Goodwin—www.reclaimyourbrilliance.com
Tai Goodwin is passionate about helping women reclaim their brilliance so they can show up as called and confident messengers, living life on their own terms.

Karyn Greenstreet—www.passionforbusiness.com
Karyn Greenstreet is committed to helping small business owners unlock their potential and create the businesses of their dreams.

Molly Gordon—www.shaboominc.com
Molly Gordon coaches others how to follow their passions, be true to themselves, and create authentic, meaningful wealth along the way.

Assessments

Gallup's Clifton Strengths Finder

www.gallupstrengthscenter.com
Identify your talents and lead with your strengths.

Personal Brilliance Quotient

www.mypersonalbrilliance.com
Learn to develop awareness, curiosity, focus, and initiative so that success—no matter how you define it—comes more easily to you.

The Fascination Advantage Test

www.howtofascinate.com
Discover how the world sees you and learn how to fascinate others.

Magazines

LiveHappy

www.livehappy.com
Join the LiveHappy happiness movement, find your happy place in all areas of life, and then impact the world through happiness.

Journals

Compendium Incorporated

www.live-inspired.com
Compendium makes a variety of journals to help you celebrate and highlight your inner thoughts.

Lovenotebooks

www.lovenotebooks.com
Lovenotebooks stocks a large collection of the world's most respected brands of day planners and notebooks.

About the Author

M. Shannon Hernandez, M.Ed., is founder of The Writing Whisperer, a college professor, and an advocate for education reform. She lives in Brooklyn, New York, with her husband, Michael, and her cat, Shakti. When Shannon is not writing, coaching, or teaching, you will find her out in the busy city streets of New York City either running or cycling.

Shannon Hernandez is available for select readings, discussion circles, and lectures. To inquire about booking an appearance, please visit www.myfinal40days.com.

CPSIA information can be obtained at www.ICGtesting.com
Printed in the USA
BVOW05s1856110814

362472BV00001B/56/P